SURVIVING LINGUISTICS

A Guide for Graduate Students

Second Edition

Monica Macaulay

Cascadilla Press   Somerville, MA   2011

Front cover photograph of the Rosetta Stone © 2006 Dave Shea

ISBN 978-1-57473-029-6 paperback
ISBN 978-1-57473-229-0 paperback 10-pack
ISBN 978-1-57473-129-3 library binding

Library of Congress Cataloging-in-Publication Data

Macaulay, Monica Ann
    Surviving linguistics : a guide for graduate students / Monica Macaulay. -- 2nd ed.
    p. cm.
    Includes bibliographical references and index.
    Summary: "A guide to graduate study in linguistics. Covers learning about graduate
school and linguistics, writing for linguists, funding and publishing research, conference
papers and posters, the dissertation, and finding a job after graduate school. Includes
exercises, references, web addresses, and index"--Provided by publisher.
    ISBN 978-1-57473-029-6 (pbk.) -- ISBN 978-1-57473-229-0 (pbk. 10-pack) -- ISBN
978-1-57473-129-3 (lib. bdg.)
    1. Linguistics--Study and teaching (Graduate)--United States. 2. Linguistics--Study and
teaching (Graduate)--Canada. I. Title.
    P57.U5M33 2011
    410.71'173--dc22

To order a copy of this book, contact:

Cascadilla Press
P.O. Box 440355
Somerville, MA 02144, USA

phone: 1-617-776-2370
fax: 1-617-776-2271
sales@cascadilla.com
www.cascadilla.com

For Joe and Becky, who helped me figure out
how to write like a linguist

Contents

Exercises

Preface

This is a book about how to become a linguist. The hidden agenda of graduate school is socialization into a professional community, and one of my goals in this book is to make some details of that process less mysterious.

I've written this book for a number of reasons. On the practical side, I teach a class at UW-Madison called "Research Methods and Materials," and the book has grown out of the readings and handouts I've prepared for it. My department decided some years back to resurrect the course (which hadn't been taught in decades) as a way of consolidating the advice the faculty found themselves giving over and over again to individual graduate students. Since there was so clearly a need for explicit instruction in matters pertaining to professionalization, especially in the area of writing, the faculty decided to formalize that instruction.

On the personal side, although I am many years past graduate school at this point, I remember all too well the frustration of trying to figure things out on my own. Most graduate advisors do their best to train their students, but often they forget just how explicit they need to be. It's easy to forget, for example, that it's not obvious how submission of abstracts works or how examples should be laid out. It's also easy to overlook the fact that many linguistics graduate students don't come into the field with a background in science, and thus aren't used to the style of argumentation and writing that is appropriate in linguistics. If you were an English major, you're probably going to write your papers like an English major would—and while you might have gotten high praise as an undergraduate, your graduate advisor in linguistics is going to be very frustrated with you until you learn to write like a linguist.

Being a graduate student in linguistics isn't easy. This book should make it a little easier.

What Counts as Linguistics?

First, as all linguists know (and have the privilege of explaining constantly), linguistics is not about learning lots of languages. So this book is not aimed at students of language(s) in that sense; it is aimed at people who work in the field of linguistics, the scientific study of language.

Having established that, I still need to say a few words on what I mean by linguistics. The terminology for explaining it is tricky. In fact, the linguistic topic of markedness arises in the very question of explaining what I mean. I do the kind of linguistics that some people call "core linguistics" (i.e., descriptive/ theoretical), but calling it that has unkind implications for any area not included in the term. There was a period when people talked about "linguistics" vs. "hyphenated linguistics" (e.g., what they used to write as "socio-linguistics"), but that was dropped because of the marginalizing effect it had on the hyphenated fields. Then there's always the vague term "applied linguistics," which commonly means the study of second language acquisition, but can refer to various other areas as well.

My goal in this book is to cover as broad a range of areas as possible, but there are numerous problems (both in terminology and content) in doing so. Because I haven't been able to find a term for the kind of linguistics which I do (and which I therefore know best) which is not (a) potentially offensive to others ("core linguistics") or (b) cumbersome ("descriptive/theoretical"), I will use the term "linguistics" both for the field in general and in some cases for the kind of linguistics that I do.

These issues arise because the different areas have different norms and conventions. This is most obvious in two areas: the distinction between qualitative and quantitative research, and the kind of format used for writing up the results of the research. This book covers both sides of both areas, hopefully without any terminological offense.

Who This Book Is For

As the subtitle indicates, this book is written primarily for graduate students. The content derives from my experiences in universities in the United States, and some sections provide advice specifically for linguistics students in the United States. While terminology and titles vary in other countries, most of the material in the chapters about the field of linguistics and about writing, publishing, and presenting papers at linguistics conferences should be useful for linguistics students in any country.

Both MA and PhD students should find the book helpful, although of course some chapters (especially chapter 9 on academic jobs) pertain more to doctoral students than Master's students. The content of chapter 8 on writing a dissertation can easily be applied to writing a Master's thesis.

Undergraduates who are considering graduate school in linguistics will find chapter 1 to be the most directly relevant for their immediate goals.

Always Ask for Advice

Everybody's experiences and perspectives are different, and consequently there may be advice in this book that you (or perhaps more importantly, your advisor) disagree with. I cannot stress enough the importance of asking lots of different people for advice. Don't let shyness or insecurity keep you from finding out the information you need, or from gaining different perspectives on a single topic. My advice in this book is derived from my experience, which may not completely correspond to what you find in your graduate program. Take everything I say with a grain of salt, and if it doesn't work for you (or if your advisor tells you something different), do things differently.

Second Edition

The second edition of this book contains lots of updates and new information, including (but not limited to!) a new section on applying to graduate school in linguistics, new book and website recommendations, more on references and citation managers, an expanded section on poster sessions, more information on getting published, and new exercises.

I've had a lot of really great feedback from readers of the first edition, and I want to thank everyone who wrote to me for their input, lots of which I have incorporated into this second edition. I did a trial run of the section on applying to graduate school with some of our (always exceptional) undergrads, and I appreciate their insights as well.

Acknowledgments

This book has even deeper roots than the class that I teach. Before I came to Madison, I taught at Purdue University, and Becky Brown, Joe Salmons, and I spent many an hour there talking about these issues. Eventually we did a workshop for the linguistics graduate students called "How to Write Like a Linguist." I am deeply grateful to Becky and Joe for all the help they have given me in thinking through my ideas on the subject. Much of what appears in this book is directly and indirectly influenced by both of them.

Many other colleagues helped me as well. Chris Golde and I had long discussions about the role of the advisor(s), as well as the process of applying for academic jobs. Monika Chavez provided me with numerous comments, especially about the section on quantitative research. Colleen Brice helped out with how things work in the world of applied linguistics. Alex Buchner told me what it was like to apply to a graduate program in linguistics in this day and age, and gave me great tips on the process. Amy Dahlstrom and my father, Stewart Macaulay, gave me extensive and detailed comments on the manuscript as a whole; and Justine Cassell, Megan Crowhurst, and Sara Trechter also provided input. Thanks also to Juliette Blevins, Johanna Nichols, Andrew Sihler, and David Silva for agreeing to let me borrow from various handouts they had prepared for their graduate students. Other colleagues to whom I am grateful for discussion and various tips include Vivian Lin and Tom Purnell, both of whom provided ideas for exercises and other suggestions. I also thank the many students who have given me insight into how to teach the kinds of things talked about in this book, especially Tammy Goss, Marianne Milligan, and Blake Rodgers.

I have participated in or been an audience member at various workshops over the years which have shaped my thinking on several of the matters discussed in this book. On the one hand there have been the professionalization workshops organized by the LSA Committee on the Status of Women in Linguistics at the LSA Annual Meeting, and I want to thank both the other participants and the audiences for the many good ideas I got from them. I especially benefited from Abigail Cohn's presentation on "Getting Grants," given at the 1999 LSA Workshop on Becoming a Professional Linguist, as reflected in the Grant Proposals section in chapter 7. There was also an interesting workshop at the 2003 LSA in which the editors of most of the major journals in the field discussed various aspects of their job. I draw on the handouts and my notes from that session in chapter 7 as well.

I am additionally indebted to the many, many books which I consulted on applying to graduate school, being a graduate student, and doing academic (and non-academic) writing. I have tried to acknowledge specific tidbits when I explicitly borrowed them, and I hope (in light of the discussion of plagiarism in chapter 3!) that I have sufficiently acknowledged all of my sources.

Finally, thank you to the anonymous reviewers of the book, and especially to Michael Bernstein at Cascadilla Press, for all of his suggestions, help, and editing.

1 Graduate School: Before, During, and After

When you start reading up on graduate school, you are likely to come across (at least) two opposing points of view about the enterprise:

> The joys of doing research are considerable, and anyone in a position to carry out research is indeed privileged. (Phillips and Pugh 2010:xvi)

> Graduate school is a ritual humiliation in which novice academics are initiated into their respective disciplines. (Peters 1997:5)

As is the case with so many things in life, most people's experience falls somewhere between these two extremes. It is indeed a privilege to spend one's time doing research, but at the same time learning the ropes is not simple or pain-free. Lesli Mitchell makes a very good point in her book on graduate school when she says, "Grad school is a career in itself" (1996:6). And just like any career, you have to learn about both the performance requirements and the social expectations of your chosen area in order to succeed at it.

Before Graduate School

This section talks about some of the issues that arise when one is thinking about going to graduate school in linguistics: taking the GRE, choosing schools to apply to, and what to put in your application.

For more information on this topic, the Linguistic Society of America (LSA) has a page titled "Graduate Study in Linguistics: Choosing a Program That's Right for You" at www.lsadc.org/info/res-gradschool-guide.cfm. Zachary Brooks has posted a very thorough exploration of applying to grad school in linguistics at applelinguist.wordpress.com/linguistics-phd-programs-application-and-review.

Your Undergraduate Major

Students who major in linguistics as undergraduates no doubt are able to focus their graduate school applications in ways that students with other majors can't. But this does not mean that you have to major in linguistics to get into graduate school in linguistics. For one thing, the field is small enough that many undergraduate institutions don't even offer a linguistics major, and admissions committees realize this. And for another, not everybody realizes that they want to do work in linguistics early enough in their college career to complete a linguistics major. Graduate students in linguistics consequently have a pretty wide variety of undergraduate majors: a particular language like French or Japanese, computer science, philosophy, and all sorts of other fields.

So, what if you've majored in something else, and now have decided to apply to graduate school in linguistics? If you're choosing to do graduate work in this field, you must already know something about it. But if you haven't done so already, take linguistics courses, read an introductory textbook and other books about linguistics, and read everything you can about the field on the web. One student of mine, for example, told me that he found Steven Pinker's various books very accessible and informative when he was trying to broaden his knowledge of linguistics before applying to grad school. The LSA also has a webpage with short descriptions of the field in general as well as of various subfields at www.lsadc.org/info/ling-fields.cfm, and some FAQs that are worth browsing through at www.lsadc.org/info/ling-faqs.cfm. Chapter 2 describes a wide range of additional resources for learning about the field of linguistics.

The Dreaded GRE

Many linguistics graduate programs require applicants to take the GRE General Test. There are GRE Subject Tests for some academic areas, but not for linguistics. Before taking the GRE, become familiar with the content and format of the test. You can raise your score and reduce your anxiety by taking practice tests, using GRE review materials, and perhaps taking a GRE class. ETS, the company that administers the GRE, has information about the test at www.ets.org/gre as well as free test prep materials.

Not all linguistics programs require the GRE, and GRE scores are only one aspect upon which applications are judged. Expectations about an applicant's scores vary depending on background—for example, non-native speakers of English may not be expected to score as highly as native English speakers. Keep in mind that admissions committees take the entire application package into account: transcript, personal statement, letters of recommendation, etc.

Choosing a Graduate Program

One of the first questions to answer is whether you should apply to an MA program or a PhD program. There are several factors to consider in making this decision. First, what are your career goals? If you're interested in teaching English to non-native speakers, an MA will probably be all you need. If you're interested in an academic career, however, you absolutely have to get a PhD. It might help to take a look at some job listings for linguists to see what qualifications are required for the different types of jobs (see www.linguistlist.org/jobs).

Second, you should check on whether the schools you're interested in even have an MA program. Many graduate programs in linguistics either don't offer an

MA, or don't accept students just for the MA degree. My program, for example, awards an MA as one of the steps to the PhD, but we don't have a separate MA program, and only accept students whose ultimate goal is the PhD.

Once you've decided on the degree you're seeking, you need to search for programs that have faculty who focus on the area you want to study. If you know exactly what you want to do, this will help narrow down the choices. But even if you don't, or only have a general idea, you can still narrow the field down by considering broader questions. For example,

- Do you want to explore a particular subfield of linguistics, like sociolinguistics or semantics?

- Is there a particular theoretical approach you're most comfortable with or want to learn about?

- Is there an applied aspect to what you're interested in?

- Are you interested in a particular language or language family?

- Are you interested in doing fieldwork or language documentation?

Figuring out the answers to questions like these will help you as you search for information on particular programs.

If you have majored in linguistics or otherwise have access to linguistics professors at your undergraduate institution, they are the best starting point for your search. Talk to linguistics faculty who you know and ask their advice. Let them know what you're interested in, and ask about programs you might apply to as well as professors they would recommend you work with. Don't be afraid to contact people they recommend—professors enjoy talking to students! Explain your interests and ask specific questions about their research, their program, and opportunities for graduate students.

Departmental websites are another good starting point. The Linguist List has a list of programs in linguistics at www.linguistlist.org/teach/programs. You'll find a lot of variation—some departmental sites are really informative and give you a nice summary of the department's philosophy and offerings, while others are less helpful.

One way to get additional information is to look at the individual pages of faculty members. Again, there's great variation in how much and what kind of information you'll find, but it's worth looking. Another good resource is individual pages of graduate students in a given program. These can provide clues to what kinds of projects are encouraged in a department. Grad student pages are often more developed and informative than faculty pages (probably because younger people tend to be more tech-savvy than older people). Try emailing some of these students, and you may get some good responses.

Here's an example of starting a search. A student recently emailed me for help finding a graduate school, and said she was interested in language and gender. I suggested that she first look for the names of scholars who work in the field and who do work that she finds interesting and exciting. I recommended looking in the journal *Gender and Language* as a way of finding such names, as well as looking at a website about language and gender by Mary Bucholtz at www.linguistics.ucsb.edu/faculty/bucholtz/lng. Finally, I suggested signing up for the International Gender and Language Association email discussion list GALA-L at listserv.linguistlist.org/archives/gala-l.html. I told her if she asked people on the list for advice they would probably be very helpful. I think the key to figuring out what programs are right for you is to cast your net very widely, and then narrow it down as you get more and more information.

The Application

As I said above, most programs take a very sensible approach and take all aspects of an application into account. Keep in mind that faculty from the program you're applying to are the ones who make decisions about admission, not a university-wide admissions committee, so you can really direct a focused narrative to them specifically. Some aspects of your application are no longer under your control (like your GPA), or only somewhat under your control (like your GRE scores), so you should concentrate on the areas that you can control.

While you're still in your undergraduate program, try to develop good relationships with at least a few of your professors. It really helps professors in the somewhat difficult job of writing recommendations if a student has made an impression. When a student that I barely know asks me for a letter of recommendation, all I can really do is say that they got such-and-such a grade in my class, but that I don't know much more about them than that. But if a student has come to my office hours, exchanged emails with me, participated in class discussions, and otherwise made an impression on me, then I have something to say, and the letter is much, much stronger.

Finally, the personal statement: these are always really, really tough to write—and especially tough to write well. Some departmental websites have very detailed advice on the personal statement (also known as the "statement of purpose"). Here are a few common recommendations:

- Describe your familiarity with the field. If you majored in linguistics, that's great, because you'll probably have a lot of experiences to draw on. Discuss your favorite classes, describe papers you've written, and mention any research you've been involved with. If you didn't major in linguistics, explain how you learned about the field, what draws you to it, and what relevant reading you've done or courses you've taken. Make it clear that you know what graduate study in linguistics is about.

- Describe your intellectual interests in general, and your interests in the field more specifically. If you have ideas about what you'd like to do research on, include that.

- What other qualifications do you have? Do you have work experience that taught you something valuable? Have you done any teaching or tutoring? Discuss any practical experience that helped mold you, even if it isn't directly relevant.

- Tailor your statement to each program you apply to. Many sites emphasize the fit between applicant and program as one of their highest priorities. Mention faculty members you would like to work with and discuss aspects of the program that really attract you.

- If there's something in your academic record that you're not too proud of, sometimes the best approach is to bring it up instead of pretending it's not there. It's certainly acceptable to say something like "my GPA isn't as high as it should be because I had a difficult semester early on in my college career. But as you can see from my transcripts, I was able to turn things around and have finished up with excellent grades." Don't dwell on whatever it is, and don't make excuses. Mention it briefly and move on to discussion of your strengths.

Visiting Prospective Programs

If at all possible, go visit the places where you're thinking of applying or have applied. Get in touch with the department chair or a professor you're interested in working with and make an appointment to talk to them while you're there. It can help to get in touch with some of the program's current graduate students too (remember, they often have a presence on the departmental website, so it should be easy to find their email addresses).

Some departments actively recruit graduate students, and invite a set of applicants to come visit (often on the department's dime, in fact). Either way, you should prepare a list of questions to ask such as the following:

- What is the funding situation for graduate students? Find out about fellowships, TAships, and research assistantships. Is there guaranteed funding? If there is, what type of funding and for how long?

- What is the average time to degree (i.e., the number of years students take to get their degrees)?

- What is the cost of living like in the area, and what is the housing situation? Is there graduate student housing? Is there anything else you should know about life in their city?

- If relevant, ask about family life and child care for graduate students.
- Is there a graduate student organization at the university or department level? What is the grad student community like?

You should already be familiar with the requirements of the program. Think carefully about those requirements and see whether you have any further questions about them.

While you're talking to the graduate students, keep in mind that a grad student's social life is very different from an undergraduate's. Most grad students don't take many courses outside their own department, and over the course of their graduate career become more and more focused on their own research, so it's much harder to be a part of the wider college community. It's not impossible to meet grad students from other departments, but it often takes some conscious effort. So make sure that you find a program with students that you feel comfortable around.

Resources

The best way to succeed at any undertaking is to know how to find out about that undertaking. The next several sections discuss people and books that you can go to for guidance (both personal and professional) before, during, and after graduate school.

Advisors

In many fields, graduate students know who they plan to work with before they start a graduate program. This is sometimes true in linguistics, but it is by no means the case for everyone. Many linguistics graduate students don't necessarily know ahead of time what area of linguistics they will wind up specializing in, so they can't really pick an advisor before learning something about the field. Instead, linguistics graduate students often wind up working with the person in their department whose specialty they develop an interest in. (Even those who think they do know ahead of time may find themselves changing their minds about their area of specialization and thus have to change to a more appropriate advisor after some period of time.) Most linguistics departments are small enough that your choice of a subfield often determines who your advisor will be, or at least narrows it down considerably.

Some programs pair incoming students with initial advisors and then expect them to choose a permanent advisor at some designated time. Our program assigns all new students to the department chair, and then at the end of the first year requires them to make a more permanent choice. This kind of switch, of course, is much easier than making a change later in one's graduate career, but you should remember that even that can be done if necessary.

Your advisor is someone who will work with you during your graduate career, and will remain (as mine pointed out to me) your advisor for life. Even after you're finished with your degree, you will need to turn to your advisor for little things like letters of recommendation and major things like career advice. So it's very important to choose the right person as your advisor.

Most of the "how to be a graduate student" books that I'm familiar with stress the importance of finding a Big Name to work with. The rationale is that when you go on the job market, prospective employers will look at who your advisor was and judge you accordingly. This is undoubtedly true, and it doesn't hurt to consider such factors as the person's area of research, publication record, and reputation. Nonetheless I have two reservations about this advice. First, prospective employers will look at many other things besides the name of your advisor: they will look at the quality of your work, where you have published, and what you have accomplished. Second, having Dr. Bigshot as your advisor will be useless to you if Dr. Bigshot happens to be one of those people who does not think it worth their while to spend time helping graduate students develop their skills. If Dr. Bigshot never reads your papers, or routinely humiliates you in public, it is not worth being associated with his or her name. So use your common sense: balance the advantage that a big name can bring you with the degree of care and help that you get.[1]

Keep in mind that you are not married to your advisor. If things aren't working out, you don't have to hire a lawyer—you can just find another advisor. Your graduate career can stall or be needlessly difficult if you remain in an advising relationship that is not giving you what you need. You're not trapped: you're an adult, and you can make a change if things are not going well. Keep in mind that your advisor is also an adult (or at least should be), and that they will probably not be offended if you switch to someone else. (In fact, they may secretly be relieved.) Don't get me wrong—it is likely to be tough on you if you make a switch in mid-stream. You will have to adapt, and may have to change your focus to some degree, but you should balance that against the problems that a bad advising situation can cause you.

Finally, remember that your advisor is not the only person who will advise you. Although that person should be a central figure in your graduate career, it is preferable to think in terms of teams of advisors. The most obvious example of this is your dissertation committee—although not everyone on the committee will necessarily read your dissertation until you have a completed draft, you should be meeting with them regularly for advice and discussion of your topic. In addition to this, however, you should be developing relationships with other professors throughout your graduate career. Some will be professors who you have taken

---

1. One option for compromise if you are unable to find these characteristics in a single person (and if your department allows it) is to have co-advisors: one whose name you can rely on and one whose advice you can rely on.

classes from, but don't discount others. If you learn of a faculty member in another department (or, for that matter, at another university) whose research is of interest to you, get in touch with them. When I was in graduate school, there was a well-known professor at another institution who was the expert in one of the areas I was writing my dissertation on. With much trepidation I wrote to him and asked if he would be willing to read something I had written. He replied immediately that he would, and wound up giving me a lot of valuable advice, and has remained a friend ever since. Sometimes such attempts may prove unsuccessful, but other times they can provide you with a contact who continues to provide support throughout your entire career.

You can also learn a lot from your fellow graduate students (see below), and from students in other departments. Since part of the advising that you will need involves the practical side of graduate school (such as understanding the requirements for graduation), the department staff will also play a role in advising you as you proceed through your program.

Your Peers

Develop a group of linguist friends who you can ask to read your papers, and return the favor. Spend time with them discussing linguistics—even though they're beginners too, they're smart beginners and can help you develop your understanding of the field. The process of working out your thoughts in this way can prove invaluable. When you're giving a conference paper, do a trial run in front of your group—it's nice to do it in front of an audience composed of friends first.

Your graduate school peers also function as a support group. You probably had a group of non-linguist friends when you came to graduate school, and they will try to support you, but if they aren't in a similar situation they won't understand the peculiar stresses you're under. Developing another group of friends among your peers will provide you with a much-needed place to blow off steam. Nobody will understand your frustrations quite as well as others who are going through the same thing, with the same hurdles and the same cast of characters.

Sometimes I hear about graduate programs where the students consider themselves to be in competition, rather than being fellow travelers on a difficult journey. I think this is a real shame, because your fellow students may prove to be the most valuable asset you have in graduate school. Don't underestimate the ways in which other students can help you out.

Book and Website Recommendations

There are many useful books and websites on writing out there, and tons on how to be a graduate student. Here are a few that I recommend:

Graduate School

The Ultimate Grad School Survival Guide
Lesli Mitchell, 1996
This book covers graduate school from the moment the idea enters one's head to the point of the post-dissertation job search. It has a breezy, readable style, and offers very concrete advice (for example, a month-by-month preparation guide for taking the GRE). A nice feature is the quotes from graduate students that illustrate the unexpected and sometimes more personal aspects of graduate school.

Getting What You Came For:
The Smart Student's Guide to Earning a Master's or Ph.D., revised edition
Robert L. Peters, 1997
This book also covers graduate school from A to Z. It treats all of the topics one would expect, such as time management, oral exams, stress, academic politics, and the dissertation. What sets it apart is its chillingly realistic tone: Peters is so honest about the difficulties of graduate school that some readers may find it discouraging. I think it's important to know the harsh realities ahead of time, though, in order to prepare yourself.

How To Get a PhD:
A Handbook for Students and Their Supervisors, 5th edition
Estelle M. Phillips and Derek S. Pugh, 2010
Because this is written for the British system, some of the content of this book will not be relevant to North American graduate students. Nonetheless, the authors have lots of good advice.

At Cross Purposes: What the Experiences of Today's Doctoral Students Reveal about Doctoral Education
Chris M. Golde and Timothy M. Dore, 2001
www.phd-survey.org
This is an extremely useful website which reports the results of a survey of graduate students from 11 different fields in arts and sciences. In addition to the results of the survey, the site includes advice for prospective doctoral students, and a page with quotes from the students surveyed answering the question, "Knowing everything that you know now, what advice would you give others entering or in the early years of graduate school?"

"So long, and thanks for the Ph.D.!"
Ronald T. Azuma, 2000
www.cs.ucla.edu/~palsberg/azuma.html
This website has the subtitle "Everything I wanted to know about C[omputer] S[cience] graduate school at the beginning but didn't learn until later," but I've heard from a number of linguistics graduate students that it was very relevant to them too.

Research, Writing, and Publication

Practical Guide to Syntactic Analysis, 2nd edition
Georgia M. Green and Jerry L. Morgan, 2001
The first half of this book considers issues such as finding a topic, making a hypothesis, argumentation, and some general strategies for writing. The focus is on syntax, but the topics covered are relevant to any area of linguistics.

Qualitative Methods in Sociolinguistics
Barbara Johnstone, 2000
Although this is a book aimed at sociolinguists, the author discusses research, data, and methodology in a way that all linguistics students can benefit from. I highly recommend the chapters on "Thinking about Methodology" (especially the section titled "What is Research?") and "Writing," in which the author lays out steps for writing an article based on qualitative research. She also has a very nice discussion of introductions in the latter chapter.

Writing an Applied Linguistics Thesis or Dissertation:
A Guide to Presenting Empirical Research
John Bitchener, 2010
This book walks the reader through the parts of an applied linguistics thesis, with a chapter devoted to each of the usual sections in such a thesis. It is very methodically written and presented, and should be helpful to those writing applied linguistics papers as well as theses.

Analyzing Streams of Language:
Twelve Steps to the Systematic Coding of Text, Talk, and Other Verbal Data
Cheryl Geisler, 2004
This is a book aimed at researchers in a wide range of fields: management research, rhetoric and composition, and presumably linguists as well. It would be especially helpful for those interested in areas like discourse or conversation analysis.

Bird by Bird: Some Instructions on Writing and Life
Anne Lamott, 1994
Students are often surprised when I assign a book on fiction writing in my research methods class, but this wonderful book is the best I've ever read on the topic of writing.

Writing for Social Scientists:
How to Start and Finish Your Thesis, Book, or Article, 2nd edition
Howard S. Becker, 2007
You'll notice as you read on that I quote this book a lot—I really like its conversational style and the practical advice that Becker gives. It's not so much a how-to type of book as an interesting discussion of issues that arise as grad students learn how to write in the social sciences.

Handbook for Academic Authors, 5th edition
Beth Luey, 2010
This is really a book for beginning professors rather than graduate students, but it has some useful material for advanced grad students in it as well. It covers topics like writing a scholarly article, turning a dissertation into a book, and editing a collection of articles. The chapter on journal articles is quite useful, and contains a nice discussion of how to choose the appropriate journal to submit to. The annotated bibliography of books on writing and other aspects of the academic life is also worth looking at.

Surviving Your Dissertation:
A Comprehensive Guide to Content and Process, 3rd edition
Kjell Erik Rudestam and Rae R. Newton, 2007
As the title says, this book is entirely about writing a dissertation. It covers aspects of research design and writing in great detail, and also includes a chapter on the social and emotional side of the process.

University of Wisconsin Writing Center Writer's Handbook
www.wisc.edu/writing/Handbook
I'm partial to the UW's online handbook, but there are many other online writing resources—most writing centers have a website these days. Surf around and you will no doubt find other very useful sites.

Academic Careers

The Chicago Guide to Your Academic Career
John A. Goldsmith, John Komlos, and Penny Shine Gold, 2001
This is one of the few guides that contains advice specific to the field of linguistics, but it isn't written in the usual how-to format. Instead, it takes the form of a conversation between three scholars from three different fields (linguistics, economics and history, and medieval history and women's studies). As such, it is much more readable than most guides, but some may find it less specific and thus less helpful than the typical graduate school guide.

The Compleat Academic: A Career Guide, 2nd edition
John M. Darley, Mark P. Zanna, and Henry L. Roediger III (eds.), 2004
This book is a collection of articles edited by a set of psychology professors, but most of the advice it gives is quite relevant to our field as well. The second edition adds a section on graduate school, and expands its coverage for new assistant professors. The section on "Research and Writing" is geared towards doing psychological research (and so setting up a lab is a major focus), which may or may not be relevant to the kind of linguistics you plan on doing. The book also contains a useful section on "Diversity in Academia."

Imposter Syndrome

If you're in graduate school, it is highly likely that you were a smart kid. You probably got very good grades, and probably didn't have to try very hard to be the best in your classes. Then . . . you get to graduate school and suddenly you're not the smartest person in the class any more. You're surrounded by smart people. This can be a shattering experience for entering grad students, as they try to find their place in a very different environment than they are used to.

But it doesn't end there. Many graduate students have a persistent feeling that they are hiding the shameful secret of how unutterably stupid they are. They feel like everybody else is smart, and they are the only dumb one in class. Often students live in fear of being found out—a common nightmare is that some day the admissions committee is going to realize that they sent the wrong letter, and that the student was only admitted by accident.

One result of this feeling is that students become afraid to speak up in class for fear of revealing themselves as the frauds they are certain they are. Another result can be excessive perfectionism, which can lead to an inability to complete projects. These kinds of behaviors can be very damaging to one's graduate and post-graduate career, and sadly are more common than you might think.

In fact, this is so common that it has a name: Imposter Syndrome. Most academics suffer from it at one point or another in their careers, and many never overcome it. (I won't name names, but a well-known professor in another field told me that at age 73 he was still waiting to get over it!) I had a pretty bad case of it writing this book—I had the sense that readers were going to be looking at my every sentence, thinking, "And *she* thinks *she* can tell *us* about writing?!?" In fact, the psychological literature is filled with studies that describe students, professors, CEOs, nurse practitioners, and others as suffering from this syndrome. It is more prevalent in women and members of minority groups, but is certainly not confined to them. Harvey and Katz (1985:3) estimate that 70% of the working world feels this way at least some of the time. If you find yourself experiencing such feelings, keep in mind that it's a very common reaction to the stress of graduate school. Talk to your fellow students, and you'll probably find out that they feel the same way. If it really becomes a problem for you, get some counseling—a trained counselor can help you to understand that you really do deserve to be where you are.

Funding

Graduate school can be expensive, and, given rising tuition costs throughout the country, will only become more so. One consideration in picking a department, then, is the funding that they can provide. There are several types of funding available in graduate school, and I review the major categories here. Note, though, that different institutions have different names for the various categories, so you will have to do a little investigation of the topic at each place you apply.

Fellowships

Fellowships generally provide the student with tuition and a stipend (usually in the form of a monthly check). Some departments control their own fellowships; at other places they are awarded by the university or college. There is no work required beyond the work of being a student, although some fellowships require that you be enrolled for a certain number of courses or credits. There are also a few graduate fellowships available which are not tied to a particular institution, such as the National Science Foundation's (www.nsf.gov) Graduate Research Fellowships and Doctoral Dissertation Improvement Grants.

Teaching Assistantships (TAships)

A Teaching Assistant (TA) is paid to teach, as the name suggests. In some cases the TA is responsible for an entire course, while in other cases the TA teaches a discussion section for a larger class with the main lectures being taught by a professor. A situation somewhat between these two extremes is often found in language departments, where the TA is responsible for an entire class, but course content and assignments are determined by a coordinator (either a faculty member, an academic staff person, or a senior TA).

Usually only senior graduate students are assigned courses of their own.[2] If you find yourself in this situation, be sure to consult extensively with faculty who have taught the course (or a similar course) before. They will have invaluable advice on choosing a textbook, designing the syllabus, determining assignments, and grading. While this kind of teaching assignment is a huge amount of work, it is great experience and looks very good on your CV when it comes time to look for a job. (CV stands for Curriculum Vitae—see chapter 9.) Generally students who get this kind of position are dissertators, though, and so must weigh the advantages that the experience will give them against the loss of writing time that it will entail.

Whether your TAship is the type where you teach your own class or the type where you assist a professor, the kinds of responsibilities you will have are likely to include (at least) class preparation, leading discussion sections or teaching your own class, preparing assignments and exams, and grading them. Universities have historically been very bad about training graduate students to teach, but this is changing.[3] In addition to specific TA training, many universities also have an on-campus resource center for teaching which may run workshops, have a library of teaching resources, or offer other help to the beginning instructor. Seek out

---

2. In some universities such assignments come with a different title, such as Lecturer.

3. My TA training (in the early 1980s) consisted of the professor for the course telling me to do whatever I wanted to do in the sections I was assigned. This would count as insufficient training.

whatever training and resources your institution and department offer, and make use of all of it.

If you're teaching small sections of a large class, consult with the professor in charge, and if they don't arrange regular meetings with you, request such meetings. Make sure that the expectations for grading are clear and consistent, to minimize disputes with students over grades (students can be incredibly cranky on this topic). Also ask the professor teaching the course (or perhaps your advisor if you're teaching your own course) to come and observe your teaching at least once. Although observations are always a bit nerve-wracking, there are two good reasons to do this: first, you can get valuable feedback on your teaching and improve aspects that need improvement. Second, the faculty member who observes you can write up a set of comments and (assuming they're favorable) can then refer back to the write-up or even enclose it when writing letters of recommendation for future teaching jobs.

Project and Research Assistantships (PAships and RAships)

This is an area where universities differ quite a bit in job titles and requirements, so I will address these two types of position together. At the University of Wisconsin, where I teach, the two are differentiated as follows: a PAship is a position in which a student assists a professor with a research project, while an RAship is the same type of position, but restricted to cases where the work has direct relevance to the student's dissertation. Other institutions may not make this distinction, may have other titles for this kind of work, or may make yet other distinctions, so you should check how things work where you are.

The duties involved can really be anything the professor can think of: working in a lab, collecting and/or analyzing data, designing a database, entering data, compiling bibliographies, collecting the materials in a bibliography, summarizing those materials, etc. These positions are distinguished from TAships simply by virtue of the fact that they do not involve teaching.

Working on a professor's project has many advantages. It can function as a sort of apprenticeship, in which you observe the process of doing research and thus fine tune your own research skills. When the topic of the project aligns with your interests, it can lead to coauthored articles, spin-off projects of your own, and in some cases even a dissertation topic.

Job Prospects Post-Degree

I always like to ask other linguists how they discovered linguistics and how they got into the field. (The Linguist List has a collection of such stories at www.linguistlist.org/studentportal/linguists/index.cfm.) I've found that many of us had a *Eureka!* moment when we realized that this was what we wanted to do for the rest of our lives. I certainly did. I took my first linguistics class in an

English department because I read the course description and thought, mistakenly, that it might help me with my crossword puzzles (an obsession at the time). I loved it, and when I found out at the end of the semester that there was a whole department devoted to the topic, I knew I had found my major.

After a semester of classes in the linguistics department, I was ready to declare my major. The undergraduate advisor conducted our conversation while talking to someone else on the phone, and the only question he asked me was, "You do know that there aren't any jobs in linguistics, don't you?" It was a little off-putting, to say the least.

I tell this story, though, to make the point that you have to have a passion for linguistics to be in this field. It isn't one of those fields, like law or engineering or business, where you come out with a degree that will make you qualified for a particular type of job. An undergraduate degree in linguistics is a very useful degree, but there is no single obvious job category into which its holder falls. An MA in linguistics can be useful in certain areas, like TESOL (Teachers of English to Speakers of Other Languages), but again, its usefulness is not as clear-cut as that of other degrees. And although some people with PhDs are able to find positions as professors of linguistics, the market is very tight, and you simply can't count on getting such a position.

So should you give up and apply to law school? Well, you have to think about it carefully. If you like linguistics but don't really love it, you probably should do something else. An important point for PhD candidates relative to this is discussed by John Goldsmith in Goldsmith et al. (2001:11): quite simply, being in academia isn't easy. Graduate school can pose hugely difficult hurdles, the so-called "two-body" issue can arise,[4] and then there's tenure to deal with if you manage to get an academic job. But if you have that passion for the field, if you know that this is what you want to do with the rest of your life (or at least for a certain period of time), then stick with it.

Golde and Dore's survey of graduate students at www.phd-survey.org found that students in PhD programs (especially those in the humanities) have very unrealistic ideas about their future. As the authors put it, "Unmistakably, the vast majority of students enter a doctoral program with a faculty career in mind" (Golde and Dore 2001:6). Yet it is common knowledge that we are graduating more PhDs than there are faculty positions available, resulting in certain disappointment for many of those graduates.

The solution is to think creatively about job opportunities and to keep your options open. Planning ahead for alternative employment is not equivalent to giving up the dream of being a professor; it's just insurance against the bad job market in academia. "The graduate students of today . . . must begin by understanding the changes in career options, not in the negative sense of a 'PhD

---

4. This is when both members of a couple—whether the second is in academia or not—hope to find jobs in the same geographical area.

glut' but in the positive sense of broadened opportunities" (Fischer and Zigmond 1998:31). That is, you may eventually decide (or know from the beginning) that a faculty position is not even what you want, especially considering what Golde and Dore describe as "the problematic nature of the tenure process, onerous workload expectations, difficulty of obtaining research funding, and low salaries" (2001:9).

A wise approach to your future career, then, is to prepare yourself by taking classes outside of your specific area of linguistics that will make you eligible for a wider range of jobs. One obvious choice would be computer science courses, since that industry is one of the major areas where linguists find jobs outside of academia.

There are various places where you can learn about careers which are available to people with degrees in linguistics. Oakland University's Linguistics Department has put together a set of resources about career opportunities with a linguistics degree at www.lin.oakland.edu/careers.html. Also try browsing the job listings on the Linguist List website at www.linguistlist.org/jobs and you will see a range of possibilities. And don't forget to talk to your advisor, other faculty members, and other linguists to get their advice.

There are also books on searching for jobs outside academia, such as Basalla and Debelius (2007), which has the delightful title *"So What Are You Going to Do with That?" Finding Careers Outside Academia*. They give very practical advice (like how to turn an academic CV into a résumé), but also focus on how to reimagine yourself in a life outside of academia. Especially helpful is their point that there is no "universal Plan B that will accommodate all of us" (2007:9); each individual has to navigate their own way through the decision-making process about life after graduate school.

To sum up, there are two things to remember: first, plan ahead, and second, be flexible. Don't let yourself think that the only possible or respectable job for you is an academic one. You may get one (if it's even what you want), but if not, there are many, many other options available.

Exercise 1: Advice on Graduate School

1. Put together a short annotated list of three websites with advice on writing, research, or graduate school that you think are particularly useful. Combine your list with the lists from other students.

2. Google "Imposter Syndrome" (also spelled "Impostor Syndrome") and see what fields are discussed in addition to the ones mentioned in this book. Summarize the advice you find on overcoming Imposter Syndrome.

3. Work together with other students in your class to come up with a list of sources of support for graduate students in your program. What fellowships can graduate students apply for? What kinds of assistantships are available? What about student hourly jobs? Is there a centralized listing of available positions?

Exercise 2: Jobs outside of Academia

The goal of this exercise is to make you aware of the opportunities that are out there, and of the fact that there are lots of jobs you could get with a PhD in linguistics besides being a professor.[5] You can do this exercise on your own or in a group with fellow graduate students. In a group, you can each look into different areas and share what you learn.

1. Write down all the possible non-academic jobs for people with a PhD in linguistics that you can think of. Then check the job listings on the Linguist List and make a more complete list.

2. Choose a particular type of job and do some background research on it. Answer such questions as: What kind of degree is needed for this job? If a PhD in linguistics is necessary, what other qualifications (if any) are needed? What kinds of companies offer such jobs? Where are these companies located?

3. Contact people who have jobs in industry and talk to them about their careers. (If you need help locating such people, ask your professors if they know any linguists you could contact who have jobs outside of academia.) Find out what you would need to do now in order to qualify for a job like theirs later.

---

5. I've modified this exercise from one that Nigel Goldenfeld (2004) describes as an exercise that he assigns to his doctoral students in physics.

2 The Field of Linguistics

This chapter provides a bit of background on the field of linguistics, from types of writing that linguists do to ways of learning about the field. Getting connected and getting a sense of your place in the field (both you personally and your work) are very important. This will help you to start feeling like you're a linguist, rather than a linguistics student.

Types of Writing That Linguists Do

This section follows a rough progression from the kinds of things you'll have to write in graduate school to things that generally only professors write, although naturally this will vary with the individual. One general piece of advice: if you're about to embark on a new type of writing (say, your first conference abstract), it's always a good idea to ask someone to show you a successful example of that kind of writing. Ask your advisor, and ask your peers. Sometimes the more advanced graduate students will be kind enough to show you some of their work. I find it always helps to have a model.

Term Paper, Seminar Paper, Critical Review

Everybody knows what a term paper is, but making the transition from an undergraduate term paper to a graduate-level term paper or seminar paper takes some work. At the graduate level, papers are not only usually longer, but they also almost always involve some original research instead of just a summary of work that others have done. In addition, a graduate term paper has to take all (or most) of the relevant literature on the topic into account, something undergraduates aren't held to quite as strictly.

Some professors also assign critical reviews in their classes. In this type of writing the student is expected, first, to provide a summary of the arguments found in a given paper. This is not to be confused with a play-by-play rehash of everything in the article—it's intended to be a synthesis. The second component to a critical review is a critique of the arguments found in the paper. It's important here not to confuse the disparaging sense of "critical" with the intended evaluative sense. While there may be legitimate criticisms of the author's arguments, what is expected here is a balanced evaluation of those arguments.

MA Thesis

Some programs require an MA thesis, which is like a graduate term paper, but longer. You should ask your advisor or other people in your program very specific questions about what is expected. See if you can find copies of MA theses by previous students in your program, to give you an idea of what the norms are.

Prelim or Qualifying Paper

Most programs require one or more prelim or qualifying papers (so called because they are preliminary to the dissertation or qualify you for the dissertation). Depending on your program, these may be part of a larger examination process before you move on to your dissertation, and/or may be part of earning an en-route MA. Again, you should ask your advisor and others what is expected. Prelim papers are usually like term papers, but a bit more developed. (In fact, in my experience, they almost always start out as term papers.) You should find out what the standards are in your program: is it supposed to be of publishable quality? (What exactly does this mean? Who makes the judgment?) Are you expected to actually submit it somewhere? (Some programs make this a requirement.) What kind of length is expected? (Yes, quality is more important than quantity, but if there are expectations about length, you'd better be forewarned.) Prelim papers also often grow into dissertation topics, and sometimes can be used in revised form as a chapter of the dissertation.

Dissertation Proposal or Prospectus

The dissertation proposal or prospectus is a statement of what you plan to do in your dissertation. Expectations vary widely, so as always, find out in advance what your advisor recommends. Even the required length can vary—I was surprised to hear from a friend at another university that they suggest 25 pages for the prospectus, when I generally tell my students that they should write about ten. Then I recently discovered that one of my own colleagues was telling her students that they only needed to write two. See chapter 8 for more about dissertation proposals.

Grant Proposal

A grant proposal is a bit like a dissertation proposal, in that it usually describes proposed research. Grant writing is discussed in chapter 7.

Dissertation

Dissertations are book-length works in our field. A mathematician might be able to get away with a three-page dissertation, but you can't. Go to the library or check on the web to see examples of dissertations that students in your department have produced (often a department will have its own library of dissertations somewhere too)—this will give you an idea of what previous graduate students in your program have done. I talk more about dissertations in chapter 8.

Review of Literature

A literature review can take many forms. Minimally, it must summarize the most important literature that has appeared on your topic. This can either be done in a section of a paper devoted to previous work on the topic, or piecemeal, as relevant. A more formal review of literature often appears as a chapter of the dissertation (commonly, it's chapter 2). In this case, the chapter consists of a summary, synthesis, and critique of the major works in the relevant area, often organized by claim or theoretical approach.[6]

Conference Abstract

Most conferences in linguistics make their decisions about what papers to accept based on the submission of short abstracts, rather than full papers. Most are quite specific about the precise length—one page or 500 words is common, often with a second page allowed for examples and/or references. See chapter 6 for advice on writing abstracts.

Conference Paper

A conference paper is delivered orally, and the length is determined by the time allotted (15 or 20 minutes is typical). In chapter 6 you will find a discussion of the differences between term papers and conference papers, and what you need to think about when you're reading a paper in front of an audience.

Book Review

There are at least three gradations of these: (a) a *book note* or *book notice* is a short summary of a book, usually one to two paragraphs; (b) a *book review* is longer (maybe two to four pages), and evaluates the book as well as summarizes it; and (c) a *review article* is an article-length evaluation of a book (or a series of books, or articles) which generally brings other literature and approaches to bear on the topic. Graduate students usually only write the first two types. Book reviews are discussed at the end of chapter 7.

---

6. Rittner and Trudeau (1997:116–117) bluntly point out that "the purpose of the review of literature is to examine and integrate relevant and salient literature into some kind of a coherent whole. It is not a series of book reports or article summaries."

Squib

A squib is a short paper (anywhere from one to maybe ten pages), usually tackling a very specific problem. Often a squib addresses a problem brought up in another article, and then provides an alternative analysis of that problem or brings new data to bear on it. Only a few journals publish squibs (*Linguistic Inquiry* being the prominent example), but some professors assign them as course work.

Journal Article

Journal articles can grow out of a term paper, a prelim paper, or a conference paper. They need to be polished and professional, and are (at least part of) what will get you an academic job—and later, tenure and promotion.

Monograph or Book

Monographs and books are longer than articles and either broader or deeper in scope. As a graduate student, you don't need to worry about writing these—the dissertation is enough of a challenge for most of us in the graduate school stage.

Collaborative Research

There are many benefits to working together, one of the major ones being that each author learns and gains insight from the other. Linguistics is not, in my experience, a field where ideas and results are jealously guarded secrets; in fact, brainstorming is usually encouraged.

Graduate students sometimes collaborate with their peers, and sometimes with a professor. There are even more concrete benefits to be had from doing the latter—you learn directly from an experienced writer about doing research, argumentation, writing, and the publication process.

One potentially problematic issue that can arise in collaborative research is the order in which the authors are listed on the paper. Happily, there is a conventional way around this: the authors are listed in alphabetical order, and then the first footnote says something along the lines of: "The authors' names are listed in alphabetical order, but both contributed equally to the writing of this paper."

Finally, you should be aware that there are different norms in the subfields of linguistics about the appropriateness or frequency of coauthorship. For example, it is highly common in phonetics, but less so in semantics. Ask your advisor about the norms in your area and (as always!) follow his or her advice on this matter.

Prescriptivism and the Linguist

One of the first principles you learn in introductory linguistics classes is "always descriptive, never prescriptive," meaning that we linguists are interested in describing (and analyzing and explaining) language data, rather than prescribing a "right" way to talk. Students are therefore often baffled to find me wielding a wicked red (or pink or purple) pen on their papers. How can I justify criticizing their writing when I've sworn a solemn oath never to be prescriptive?

The answer is (as it so often is) that things aren't black and white. In this case the answer lies in the difference between spoken and written language. Written language is a very different kind of construct than spoken language is, and the slogan above really only applies to the latter.[7] Writing *can* be revised, so why not revise it? Writing lasts, so why not make it as effective, concise, direct, and even aesthetically pleasing as possible?

I hasten to add that I'm not an extreme prescriptivist when it comes to writing. I sometimes use "whom" when I write (never when I speak), but frankly, I couldn't care less about most of the silly rules we're supposed to adhere to (like not ending sentences with prepositions). What I do care about is clarity. Linguistics is a field that values clarity of expression in writing: a direct statement of one's argument, and straightforward language. As the bumper sticker says, eschew obfuscation.

Charles Hockett on Clarity

Clarity is no virtue: it is the most elementary of scholarly duties. Obfuscation, on the other hand, is a sin. (Hockett 1966:73)

Learning about the Field

There are all sorts of ways in which you can learn about aspects of your chosen field in addition to the many fine books about linguistics. Websites contain vast amounts of useful information and advice. Email-based discussion lists allow you to read and participate in discussions on any area of linguistics. Professional organizations host meetings, publish journals and newsletters, and provide job announcements and other useful information. You can learn about current research and meet other linguists at conferences. And don't forget that your fellow graduate students and professors are also valuable resources. In this section I discuss some of these ways of learning about the field.

---

7. This is admittedly an oversimplification, in that adherence to prescriptive rules comes into play in the spoken language as well (even for linguists). We all control a wide variety of registers (types of speech used in different situations), and more formal registers may involve the use of more prescriptive rules than others. For one interesting perspective on this topic see Cameron (1995).

Books

The Language Instinct
Steven Pinker, 1994
This is one of the most widely-recommended books about language and linguistics, and justifiably so. It provides an accessible and clearly written introduction to the claims of modern linguistics in the Chomskyan tradition, and also addresses prescriptivism and popular misconceptions about language and language use.

The Cambridge Encyclopedia of Language, 3rd edition
David Crystal, 2010
There are a number of encyclopedias that deal with language and linguistics; this is a (relatively!) concise one that covers a huge range of topics in the field, including issues of contemporary interest like language endangerment and electronic communication. It isn't the kind of book that you read cover to cover, but rather is something you can dip into at will, to learn about specific areas that interest you.

Language Files, 10th edition
Anouschka Bergmann, Kathleen Currie Hall, and Sharon Miriam Ross (eds.), 2007
Any introductory textbook will surely give you a good overview of the field; I like *Language Files* because of the way the topics are presented in stand-alone sections. The 10th edition has been expanded and updated, and includes a chapter on what you can do with a major in linguistics.[8]

The Linguistics Student's Handbook
Laurie Bauer, 2007
This rather eclectic book has chapters on various topics of relevance to writing in the field of linguistics. Curiously, it also has chapters on how to pronounce linguists' names (including whether they're male or female) and common spelling errors. There is also an almost 150-page list of languages of the world, complete with details about their names, families, and salient features.

Electronic Resources

Here I describe just a few of the many Internet-based resources which you may find helpful. It's up to you to explore further and find others. Because website addresses do change, a regularly updated list of all website addresses listed in this book is available at www.cascadilla.com/surviving.html.

---

8. I've coauthored a pamphlet with Kristen Syrett titled "Why Major in Linguistics?" on just this topic (www.lsadc.org/info/ling-faqs-whymajor.cfm), and I am happy to see other discussions of the topic in print.

Sites of General Interest

Linguist List
www.linguistlist.org
This is the central website for linguistics in North America (and probably world-wide). It's also the home of the Linguist List's email discussion list, which at present has 27,000 subscribers. The website includes numerous informational pages, including email and web addresses of linguists, linguistics programs, and departments; links to data sources on the web; listings of currently advertised jobs plus an internship registry, and more. You can subscribe to the discussion list at the website—and I strongly urge you to do so.

The Linguist List Student Portal
www.linguistlist.org/studentportal
The student portal at the Linguist List site provides links to resources on a whole range of useful topics, including an introduction to the field itself, linguistics programs and departments, doing research, careers in linguistics, and so on.

Linguistic Fieldwork Preparation: A Guide for Field Linguists
www.chass.utoronto.ca/lingfieldwork
This site provides course syllabi, information on funding sources and technology, discussion of ethics, and a bibliography of linguistic and anthropological readings on fieldwork.

Linguistic Society of America (LSA)
www.lsadc.org
The LSA is the main professional organization for linguists in the United States. Their website contains a wide variety of useful pages covering such topics as grants, jobs, and publishers, and there is a listing of members which can come in handy for contacting other linguists. You should also be sure to read their pages on the (sub)fields of linguistics and take a look at their very helpful FAQs about language and linguistics.

American Association for Applied Linguistics (AAAL)
www.aaal.org
The AAAL is the largest society for applied linguistics in the United States. They describe themselves as "a professional society whose members use a wide variety of theoretical frameworks and methodological approaches to address a broad range of language-related issues that affect individuals and society."

Sites with a Specific Focus

Obviously there are thousands of sites I could mention here; the ones below are examples of the kinds of sites that are out there. Go forth and surf!

American Council on the Teaching of Foreign Languages (ACTFL)
www.actfl.org

Computational Linguistics
www.ai.mit.edu/projects/iiip/nlp.html

Endangered Language Fund
www.endangeredlanguagefund.org

The International Phonetic Association
www.langsci.ucl.ac.uk/ipa

Lexical Functional Grammar (LFG)
www.essex.ac.uk/linguistics/external/LFG

Rutgers Optimality Archive (ROA)
roa.rutgers.edu

Society for the Study of the Indigenous Languages of the Americas (SSILA)
www.ssila.org

Personal Webpages

Another good source of information is individual linguists' personal pages. They often have useful links, discussions of a favorite theory, course syllabi (especially useful when you are planning your own class), unpublished manuscripts (a good way to read the very latest work), and sometimes even published manuscripts as well.

Email Discussion Lists

There are many discussion lists in addition to the Linguist List. Usually these other lists are specialized by topic, theory, or language (or language family)— although there are other parameters too, as you'll see below. The following is a small sample:

Funknet
mailman.rice.edu/mailman/listinfo/funknet
This is a list for people who are interested in functional approaches to language.

Linguist List and more
www.linguistlist.org/lists
In addition to the Linguist List's own discussion list, the site also hosts and archives over 100 other specialized linguistics email lists.

Optimal List
camba.ucsd.edu/mailman/listinfo/optimal
This is a list for discussion of OT (Optimality Theory).

Gender and Orientation

There are several organizations and mailing lists specific to gender and orientation in linguistics. There's also a nice discussion of gender issues in academia in general at people.mills.edu/spertus/Gender/pipeline.html.[9]

Committee on the Status of Women in Linguistics (COSWL)
www.lsadc.org/info/lsa-comm-women.cfm
COSWL considers gender issues in linguistics and makes recommendations to the LSA. They also hold an open meeting every year at the LSA annual conference, which is a good way for female linguists to network with other women in the field.

OUT in Linguistics (OUTIL)
www.stanford.edu/~zwicky/outil
OUTIL is "open to lesbian, gay, bisexual, dyke, queer, homosexual, etc. linguists and their friends."

Women in Linguistics Mentoring Alliance (WILMA)[10]
ling.wisc.edu/wilma
WILMA is a mentoring organization for women in linguistics. Female linguists can sign up at the website to be mentored, to act as mentors, and also to set up discussion groups for topics of interest to women in the field.

Fonts

There are several phonetic symbol fonts available, and you can find links to a number of them at the Linguist List website. You will also find information at that site on fonts for non-English alphabets and transcription systems, as well as fonts for drawing syntactic and prosodic tree structures. Here are a few fonts that you may find helpful.

Arboreal
www.cascadilla.com/arboreal.html
This commercial font is commonly used for creating syntax trees.

IPAPhon
www.chass.utoronto.ca/~rogers/fonts.html
This is a downloadable IPA font designed by Hank Rogers.

---

9. An interesting publication on this topic is the 1992 handbook by the Members of the Committee on the Status of Women in the Profession of the American Academy of Religion. Although aimed at women in religious studies, it has good general advice for women in academia, from graduate school through tenure.

10. I confess that I am one of the organizers of WILMA, so my advocacy here may be a bit biased.

SIL International IPA Fonts
scripts.sil.org/FontDownloads
The most popular Unicode fonts containing phonetic symbols, Doulos SIL and Charis SIL, are available for free from SIL International. You can also find other IPA fonts there, as well as fonts for a variety of non-Latin scripts.

Other Software

LaTeX for Linguists
www.essex.ac.uk/linguistics/external/clmt/latex4ling
Linguists use all sorts of word processors to write their papers. For those who use LaTeX, this site offers advice and tools specifically for linguists.

Linguist List Text and Computer Tools
www.linguistlist.org/tools
The Linguist site provides links to dozens of computer tools for linguists.

SIL International
www.sil.org/computing/catalog
The SIL site has downloadable database management programs and many other programs to support linguistic field work.

Linguistics Fun

Robert Beard (a.k.a. Dr. Goodword) links to lots of entertaining linguistics-related items at www.alphadictionary.com/fun/fun.html. Check out the *Speculative Grammarian* at www.specgram.com for "research in the neglected field of satirical linguistics." And, whatever you do, don't write like this: www.rubberducky.org/cgi-bin/chomsky.pl.

Professional Organizations

The main organization for linguists in the United States is the Linguistics Society of America (LSA), and the main organization for applied linguistics in the U.S. is the American Association for Applied Linguistics (AAAL). There are also linguistics societies in many other countries, for example the Canadian Linguistics Association, the Linguistics Association of Great Britain, the Linguistic Society of Hong Kong, etc. In addition, just about every interest group (theoretical, language-oriented, or areal) has a society.

There are several reasons to join such societies. First, it's a way to get connected with other people who have interests similar to yours. Second, you usually have to join if you want to give a paper at the associated conference, which you will probably eventually want to do (see below). And third, often you get something nice in return, such as a journal, a newsletter, or a regular electronic bulletin. Again, the goal here is to get yourself plugged in to what's going on in the field in general, and more specifically in your area of interest.

You can find out about the many linguistics societies that are out there in various ways—the web is one obvious resource. You should also talk to your professors about what organizations they belong to, and get their advice on which would be most useful to you. Some of the organizations are fairly expensive to join, so that may affect your decision, but many have a more affordable student rate.

Conferences

So why go to conferences? One reason that ought to occur to you right away is to give papers. But then, why give papers? After all, it's torture, right? You have to stand up in front of a bunch of strangers who might rip your ideas to shreds. That's nobody's idea of fun.

There are several answers to this. First of all, you can go to conferences just to be a spectator. This is extremely valuable, especially at first, as a way to get yourself used to the idea of actually giving a paper. You can witness the rituals (those time cards) and see that it's very, very rare for a speaker to be ripped to shreds by the audience. You can also learn something. All those papers are being given for a reason: to disseminate the author's ideas about some topic. Just about every conference has some awful papers, but most have many very interesting papers which might even affect the research that you do.

A second important reason for going to conferences is to network and schmooze. You can meet people, from famous professors to other grad students, and talk about your ideas, sometimes even getting useful pointers on your research. Occasionally an editor of a journal will approach someone who has just given a paper, and suggest that they submit it for publication. This could happen to you! You can also make conference friends. Some of my best friends are people that I've met at conferences, that I only talk to on email, and that I only see once or twice a year.

Third, some organizations publish the papers which are read at their conference. Conference proceedings, as they are called, are a relatively easy way to get published, and publishing is the main element in getting jobs, tenure, and promotion. Conference proceedings are usually not weighed as heavily in such decisions as refereed journal articles,[11] but they are still an important accomplishment.

And fourth, you're going to have to get used to the idea of speaking in public. It's hard, and for some of us it never really gets any easier. But you need to get known, and you need to develop a reputation in the field (hopefully a good one), and giving papers at conferences is one of the main ways to do it.

---

11. Not sure what a refereed journal article is? See chapter 7.

Another way to pick up tips on giving talks is to go to as many of your departmental colloquia as possible. Not only will you learn something, but you will also learn how to give talks (and how not to). If your department is hiring, be sure to go to the candidates' job talks too. These are like conference talks, but substantially longer, and if you do apply for academic jobs you will be expected to give some. The best way to learn how to give a job talk is to witness a few.

Exercise 3: Finding Resources on the Web

In this exercise you will do web research to develop a comprehensive list of information relevant to a topic of interest to you, and you will see how much is out there on the web that you can make use of—always keeping in mind, of course, that information on the web is never guaranteed to be accurate. This type of list will give you a good starting point for doing real research.

1. Pick a topic that you're interested in. This could be a specific topic or any of the kinds of areas discussed above: a subfield of linguistics, a theoretical approach, a language, or a language family.

2. Start exploring the web to see what's out there on your topic. Follow any and all links to wherever they lead you. Keep a log of where you wander on the web. Note useful and not-so-useful sites.

3. Write down the names of scholars who are cited on relevant webpages or whose names crop up repeatedly. Visit the homepages of all of these people.

4. Note discussion lists having to do with your topic.

Exercise 4: Getting into Linguistics

1. Create a short annotated bibliography of three books, articles, or websites that sparked your original interest in the field of linguistics, and that you would recommend to others who would like to learn about the field but don't have any linguistics background. If you can't remember any specific sources, you could try asking fellow graduate students for recommendations.

2. If you're doing this as part of a class, combine all of your bibliographies into one big list. It'll be interesting to see if two or more people picked a particular source, and to compare what they had to say about it.

3. Distribute the combined list to everyone in the class, but also to others who might be interested. If your program has an undergraduate linguistics major, distribute it to those majors. Or put it up on your department's website. And while you're at it, send it to me at mmacaula@wisc.edu—I'm always curious to see what people find helpful.

3 Writing Basics

This chapter and the next cover the core skills that are needed to write a linguistics paper or thesis. In this first chapter on writing, I take a look at foundational issues such as where to start in finding a topic, how to do background research, and how to avoid inadvertent plagiarism. I also address nonsexist writing and the importance of obtaining informed consent for certain kinds of research.

I should stress at this point that this is not intended to be a style manual. I will make the occasional comment about stylistic issues, but you do need to buy yourself a real style manual (*The Chicago Manual of Style*, for example), and use it.

Finding a Topic

Students—especially beginning students—often come to their professors and say, "I can't think of anything to write about!" Some professors get really annoyed by this complaint, but I have to have some sympathy, since I can remember fairly clearly from my own early graduate school days the sense that I simply didn't know what made an interesting topic, or how to think of one in the first place. I think part of the problem is that students often think the way to find a topic is to sit down and concentrate really hard, and then miraculously something will appear in their brain. This doesn't usually happen. Either the idea comes to you while you're in the shower and *not* trying to think about it at all, or it comes to you because you have some prompt. This section will give you some ideas about how to prompt that brain of yours into action (for when the shower method just doesn't work).

Approach 1: Old Volumes of Journals

Presumably you know whether you want to write a paper in syntax or phonology or some other area of linguistics. Choose some of the major journals in that subfield and skim over papers in old volumes of those journals.[12] Think

---

12. Not sure what counts as a major journal in the subfield you're interested in? This is the kind of question you should ask your advisor or some other faculty member about. Don't be shy—you're not expected to know this innately.

about the data and problems that are addressed in these articles, and how they might be approached within a more modern framework. You may be able to find a topic that was handled somewhat clumsily in an old theory that could be dealt with more elegantly in a new theory. You might find an analysis that could interestingly be applied to new data, or an experiment that could be tried with a different subject population or dataset. Voilà: you've got a paper topic.

Approach 2: Reading Lists

Go over the readings for your course or choose a set of readings in some other way, and read critically. Look for inconsistent arguments, flaws in argumentation, and ad hoc solutions. If you can find some kind of serious problem in an analysis that someone else did, you have a topic. (Of course, then you have to come up with a better analysis, but that's another issue.)

Make sure that your criticisms are justified and specific. It's not enough just to say "this paper is dumb." You have to be able to explain why you think the analysis doesn't work and what's wrong with it. It's not an aesthetic opinion that you're delivering; it's a scientific judgment.

Another approach to criticizing an analysis is by finding contradictory data. Think about the analyses you're reading with respect to data in some language you know something about. If your data contradict the claims in the paper, that's interesting.

Discuss your criticisms and counterexamples with your professor(s), and see what they think. They might tell you that you're wrong, but maybe they won't. They might tell you that someone else has already made the criticism you've come up with, in which case you should find the source and read the critique. You may be back at square one, but that's okay. At least it verifies for you that you know enough to spot a flawed argument. Just keep trying until you find something nobody else has done yet.

Approach 3: Data

Instead of starting from theory, you might want to start from data. If you speak or work on a little-studied language, you have a wealth of topics right at your fingertips. But even if you prefer to work on English or some other highly-studied language, you can find a topic by observing some odd wrinkle in an overheard utterance. As you blossom into a linguist, you will gradually develop the ability to hear your own language (including your own utterances) as data, and this can be a valuable source of research topics. It's true that we may drive our friends and family crazy by paying attention to the structure of what they say rather than the content, but this is just an occupational hazard.[13]

Another possibility—and this requires a certain investment of time—is to find a grammar of an obscure language, and start trying to figure out everything you can about it. Often the older grammars are best for this, since there are almost always strange nuggets of data oddly described in them.

To discover a topic working from a set of language data, begin by working through your data thoroughly and carefully. Make charts and tables and write rules. If the language is little known, you might be able to write a purely descriptive paper. But it's more likely that you will find a topic by thinking about how the data would be analyzed in some theory that you're familiar with. Chances are you'll find something of interest this way.

Approach 4: Questions

Green and Morgan (2001:17–22) describe a method that works when you have a vague idea of a topic that you want to investigate, but can't figure out where to start or how to focus it. They suggest making a list of questions about the topic that need to be answered, and even provide a list of specific questions that you might want to run through (see Green and Morgan 2001:18). They stress the importance of making up the list as a list of questions, not statements, so that you are forced to come up with answers.

Brainstorming in this way with your fellow students (or a professor, if he or she is willing) is very useful. In this case you need to start with much more general questions than Green and Morgan suggest, since the group or person you're brainstorming with will need to be filled in on the very basics of the topic. It's the act of explaining the details that often makes one realize what's interesting about a topic. The kinds of questions I've used in doing this as an exercise with students in my class include the following (although of course not all will be relevant to all topics):

- What is the general area of the paper (syntax, morphology, phonology, . . .)?

- What is the basic research question or topic?

- What theory are you working in?

---

13. Charles Fillmore always used to carry a packet of tissues in his shirt pocket. In the good old days, these packets had a piece of cardboard in the package to hold it stiff. When he heard something that grabbed his attention, he would pull the cardboard out and write it down. Since they don't put that cardboard in tissue packets any more you will have to find other things to make notes on—paper napkins, envelopes, whatever's available. Don't just try to remember interesting utterances or ideas—I can guarantee you won't remember them accurately.

- What language or languages are you focusing on?

- Have the data already been collected, or if not, what procedure will you use to collect the data?

- Has anyone written on the topic before? If so, who, when, and where?

- What have they said about it? What kinds of analyses have been done?

- Have previous analyses been done in the same theoretical framework you're working in, or in a different one?

- What problems do you see in previous analyses?

- Are there subparts to the problem that are going to have to be explored?

The first time I did this with my class as a demonstration, the person who volunteered to be questioned said that it was very useful to her. The other students came up with questions that neither she nor I had thought of, and to which she didn't know the answers. Far from being an embarrassment, this was extremely helpful—it gave her new directions in which to take her research.

Green and Morgan also discuss the problem that students often think "all the easy stuff's already been done" (2001:17). They stress two points: first, it's not true, and second, even when a topic has been "done," it may not have been done very well. Becker agrees:

> "That's been done" very often does get said to people, . . . most often to students searching for a dissertation topic. . . . Such remarks rest on a serious fallacy: that things with the same name are the same. They aren't, at least not in any obvious way, so studying "the same thing" is often not studying the same thing at all, just something people have decided to call by the same name. (Becker 1998:89)

That is, there are always more questions one can ask about any given topic, so don't just reject topics that have long histories of analysis in the field.

Background Research

Responsible scholarship requires that you do a thorough job of background research. If you're going to write on a given topic, you absolutely have to know what others have said about it. As an undergraduate, you might have been able to get away with not knowing all the relevant literature, but as a graduate student, you can't.

One of the worst consequences of not doing your background research is the phenomenon of the reinvention of the wheel. This is when a solution to some problem is proposed that was already proposed (and possibly rejected for very good reasons) many years back. It is an embarrassment when this happens—and you don't want to be the one who suffers that embarrassment.

So how do you find out what has been done on your topic? We're not quite to the point yet where everything is on the web, so you will probably have to make some trips to the library. But a combination of web searching and library work should get you most of it.[14]

Whenever I write a paper, I start a bibliography on the topic.[15] My goal is to make it as complete as I possibly can. The actual degree of thoroughness will, of course, vary depending on what the topic is—a thorough bibliography on switch reference is much more doable than a bibliography on everything ever written on the passive, for example. If you're working on a broad topic that has been worked on extensively before, narrow it down to some relevant parameters and focus on that in your bibliography. You might just look at works within a specific theory, or in a particular language or language family, for instance. Read as much as you can—it can't hurt.[16]

It's helpful, too, to annotate your bibliography. At this point, it's just for your own use, but doing this will help you to remember what was useful in particular works, why you included particular items, and so on.

The next section looks at the resources you can use to find references on your topic. But there is one additional method that I always use: scanning the references sections of the works I've already found. Obviously by doing this you can't find anything more modern than the article or book whose references you're looking at, but you will note that certain references get repeated over and over again—a hint that those are considered the primary works on the topic. You should make sure that you address them in your paper too.

Library Resources

There are many bibliographies of works in linguistics, both in printed and electronic form, as listed below. Talk to a reference librarian about which ones your library has, and also about getting electronic access. Reference librarians are amazingly knowledgeable, and may be able to direct you to bibliographies and resources other than the ones that are listed here, especially if your topic diverges from fairly core linguistic areas.

---

14. You can also ask your professors for suggestions of work that has been done on your topic. But do that *after* you have checked the web and the library, rather than as a substitute.

15. See chapter 4 for discussion of citation managers, programs that can make keeping track of references much easier.

16. I do have to put in a word of caution here. Reading background material can become an obsession, and it can turn into a way to avoid actually doing any writing. So do read a lot, but don't let it keep you from doing your own work.

Major Sources for Linguistics

- Bulletin Signalétique 524: Sciences du Langage
- Dissertation Abstracts
- Humanities Index
- Language Teaching
- Linguistic Bibliography
- Linguistics Abstracts
- Linguistics and Language Behavior Abstracts (LLBA)
- MLA Bibliography (Part III: Linguistics)

The one that I have found most useful in my work is LLBA. Nonetheless, you should scour as many of these as possible for articles on your topic, since the different bibliographies cover different sources with only partial overlap. It gets repetitive, but is worth the effort.

The Scientific Method

Once you have a topic, and have found the relevant literature, you need to find a way to approach your topic. Luckily for us there's a standard way to deal with linguistic data: the good old scientific method.

One challenge facing some new linguistics graduate students is that they come in with a background in the humanities, rather than the sciences. This can make it difficult to adjust to the very different style of writing and argumentation that is appropriate in this field.

A fellow linguist—one who shares my concern for student writing—found a poster about the scientific method in a teachers' supply store, and I often use it to try to get the basics across. Here are the steps it lists:

Steps in the Scientific Method

- Choose a problem
- Research your problem
- Develop a hypothesis
- Figure out the procedure you will need to follow
- Test your hypothesis
- Organize your data
- State your conclusions

Right there you've got a nice recipe for how to do linguistic research. You first need to find a topic—and I've already covered that. Then you need to do research on the topic. The advice the poster gives is: "Look in books, get advice, make observations." In other words, do your library and web research, talk to your advisor and/or other professors, and start thinking about relevant data. Next you need to develop a hypothesis, which means coming up with a possible answer to the question you posed at the beginning of the process. Your hypothesis might be wrong, but that's a result too. When your hypothesis is wrong, you adjust it, and try again. That's how science progresses: we make a hypothesis, then we or others prove it wrong, and then we or others make a new hypothesis.

Don't work on your hypothesis all by yourself. Discuss it with your peers and your professors. Whatever you do, don't write up your whole paper without talking through your ideas with somebody (or somebodies). You will have wasted a lot of time if it turns out that you made one wrong assumption somewhere that ruins your whole hypothesis, and which someone could have pointed out to you earlier in the process.

In figuring out your procedures, the poster advises, "Write down *everything* you will do. Others should be able to repeat your experiment by reading your procedures." If you're doing any kind of experimental or survey work, this is a rule to live by. And if you're not doing an experiment or survey, it's still important to be explicit about the steps you take to arrive at your conclusions. Your hypothesis must be testable by others. The poster also warns, "Control your variables"—this is as important in finding or eliciting example sentences as it is in designing a questionnaire. (I talk more about examples in the next chapter.)

To test your hypothesis, you need to run your experiment, administer your questionnaire, or gather and analyze your data. The poster somewhat sanctimoniously reminds you here: "Be honest." It's good advice. You cannot succeed in linguistics or any academic or scientific field if you fake your data.

Once you've gathered the relevant information, you'll need to organize the data. I can't emphasize the importance of this enough. You will not be able to come to any kind of valid conclusions by just eyeballing your data. And skimming through your notebook twenty times to find a sentence you're positive you elicited (if you could only find it) is a huge waste of time. You'll have to organize your data into some kind of database (whether it be the old-fashioned index card kind, electronic, or something else that works for you). Then you can start playing with it, counting things, making charts and tables and graphs— whatever will help you to visualize what's going on.

As you're going over your data, think back to your beginning linguistics courses. The phonology, syntax, and morphology problems that you were most likely given contained a controlled set of data, and your task was to look for a generalization that accounted for everything you found. The generalization is the holy grail of linguistics, and the linguist's job is to find it. Your job now is exactly the same as it was in those problem sets—with one difference: the data set isn't controlled, and the data are likely to be much more messy. It's a harder task, but essentially the same approach will work.

And finally, state your conclusions. Don't beat around the bush, thinking it's better to be coy. Say what you found, and what it means.

Making an Argument

There's actually a step missing in the above list of steps in the scientific method, and this is that you usually can't just go from data to conclusions. In most linguistic work, you must argue for your conclusions. Now, if you're measuring some phonetic variable, and your paper is purely a report on those measurements, you don't really need to argue for the measurements. But this won't work for a paper providing an analysis of some syntactic construction or making a theoretical claim about some phonetic data.

Steps in an Argument

A linguistic argument contains, at the very least, the following steps: a statement of the claim being made; the introduction of supporting evidence, usually in the form of linguistic data; and an explanation of how the evidence supports the claim. Let's take a look at each step in some detail.

- **State the claim you are making**
  State your claim very explicitly. Contextualize it: what theoretical assumptions do you make? Are you looking at only one language in making this claim, or do you intend it to be universal? Is there a typological component to your claim—i.e., does your claim involve patterns across sets of languages? Does your claim contradict someone else's claim? (If so, you'll need to take some space to lay out the previous claim.)

- **Introduce supporting evidence, usually in the form of linguistic data**
  Make sure that your data really support your claim. This may sound so obvious that it's absurd, but it's something that people do slip up on. Under this heading you can also introduce quotes from other authors, cite data from others' work, and so on. Just be sure that everything you put in is relevant, or it will actually detract from your argument.

- **Explain how the evidence supports your claim**
  After you've introduced your evidence, you have to explain why it's relevant. Be explicit. Walk the reader through the data and then *explain* how the data support the claim. Don't assume it will be obvious to the reader—it may not be.

Most papers will have a single, central claim, supported by various kinds of evidence, so the last two steps may be repeated several times. The more distinct arguments you can make for your claim, the stronger the claim becomes. Just be sure that you're not being repetitive, and that your arguments are solid.

A common addition to the steps above is the development of several alternative hypotheses to explain the data. These competing hypotheses are compared, and one is chosen as better than the others. The decision about which is best is based on a principle known as Occam's Razor, which boils down to choosing the simplest explanation. Linguistics, like other sciences, values simplicity and parsimony in explanation. So, for example, an explanation which involves one principle is valued more highly than one which involves two principles (all other things being equal).

Another addition to the above list arises in certain sorts of theoretical arguments, where you need to explore the predictions that a claim makes. If you claim that a particular analysis of a given set of data is the right one, that may make predictions about the correct analysis of other data, which then need to be checked. If the predictions hold, this is good support for your claim.

Mistakes to Avoid

- **Don't confuse the notion of making an argument with the notion of having an argument**
  You're not arguing *with* somebody about your claim; you're arguing *for* a claim. It may be true that part of what you want to do in your paper is contradict someone else's claim, but that's a separate issue from arguing for your claim. See "Discussing the Opposition" on page 42.

- **Don't present supporting data without explaining why the data support the claim**
  Explicitness is considered a virtue in linguistic writing. As I said above, don't assume that the point of a set of data is so obvious that it does not bear repeating. Explain every single example.

- **Don't argue against a straw man**
  A straw man (perhaps I should call it a "straw person") is a position that an author sets up purely for the purposes of tearing it down. The worst form of straw man argumentation is to ascribe a position or claim to some author which is not in fact what that author said. If X is a misrepresentation of someone's position, or if X is a claim that no reasonable person would ever make, then you're wasting your time arguing against X.

- **Don't hedge**
  Hedges are expressions like "I think," "it seems," "it appears," "it might be," "sort of," "maybe," etc. These undermine your argument, and should be avoided. If you're not sure about your claims, you shouldn't be writing about them. It's as simple as that. Nonetheless, most of us still can't help putting hedges in, and this is one place where your editors can really help you: tell them to be ruthless about taking the hedges out. When I write, I'm acutely aware of the hedges I put into my statements, since I've thought so much about the topic of writing. But sometimes I just can't help myself—

and one of my editor's major jobs when he reads over my work is taking them out. Try to be aware of them, try to avoid them, and then make sure you have someone else read your work to take out the ones that slipped in anyway.

- **Don't claim something is an argument when it's really only an observation**
  I often see a real misuse of the word *argue* in student papers. The usual pattern is to give some data, point out something factual about the data, and then later in the paper incorrectly say, "I argued above that the data show X." Be sure that when you say you argued for something, you really did.

A Final Note about Argumentation

Perlmutter (1974:83) points out that learning argumentation is actually more important than learning the specifics of some theoretical position, in that the specifics will change over time, while the mode of argumentation stays the same. This is not to say that you don't have to learn the specifics, but just that you have to realize and remember that those specifics are only as good as the arguments they are based on. The best way to learn linguistic argumentation is to read a lot of linguistics. When you read, pay attention to the way that the authors argue for their points, as well as to the points themselves. Observe how they present their hypotheses, how they present the data, and how they compare competing hypotheses. After a while argumentation should become second nature to you.

Respect

Discussing the Opposition

It's very common for younger scholars to relish the idea of ripping into someone else's work, and to go overboard in doing it. But trust me on this one: if you do this, you'll regret it later on in life. It's not that you can't disagree with other authors; in fact, that's what a great deal of the literature in any field involves. But you have to learn to express your disagreements respectfully. The authors in question didn't make the claims they made because they are idiots; they made their claims based on some sort of evidence and some sort of argumentation. If you think they were wrong, show where they went wrong, but don't insult them. Even if you privately do think someone is an idiot, keep it to yourself.

Nonsexist Writing

Nonsexist writing is important both in the text and in the example sentences. Within the text, the main issue that arises for linguists is pronominal usage, and there is a set of common ways to handle this (e.g., the use of a plural pronoun or *he or she* rather than a masculine pronoun). But it is the example sentences that can really get us in trouble. In fact, Colleen Brice and I coauthored a paper (Macaulay and Brice 1997) on the results of a study we did of the example sentences in eleven syntax textbooks, where we found an enormous amount of gender bias and stereotyped behavior represented. We linguists often don't think about the content of example sentences, but their content is very salient to readers.

Why should you care about nonsexist writing? A good selfish reason is that many other people care, and if you use a style (say, the so-called "generic *he*") that offends some of your readers, you will distract their attention from the content of your work to the style of your work.[17] A more general reason is that study after study has shown that some readers do feel excluded by writing that uses sexist language and forms. That is, these really do have effects on readers, both direct (the sense of exclusion) and indirect (the annoyance factor). No matter what your political stance on the subject, your goal should be to get as many people as possible to appreciate your research—and avoiding sexist language is one way to avoid alienating a large part of your potential audience.

The LSA (among many other professional organizations) has adopted guidelines on nonsexist writing—see www.lsadc.org/info/lsa-res-usage.cfm.[18]

Plagiarism

Plagiarism is a tough topic to talk about. The minute it's raised, students start feeling defensive, as if they are being accused of something. But it's critically important to understand what counts as plagiarism, and even the most scrupulously honest student may not understand the fine points.

Some studies have shown that international students have a harder time avoiding plagiarism than North American students do (e.g., Wang 1997, Deckert 1993), but other studies throw some doubt on those claims. This is the first issue that I address here. Most North American students think that they already know what plagiarism is, but nonetheless everyone should read the second section below about various types of plagiarism. The antidote to plagiarism, paraphrasing, is addressed in the third section below with examples.

International Students and the Cultural Explanation

In the North American context, plagiarism is considered a form of cheating which can get you an F in a course, or worse, get you kicked out of school. The vast majority of professors will react with fury when confronted with what they

---

17. Of course, this is also why we follow prescriptive grammatical rules in writing.

18. The American Philosophical Association has a more extensive set of guidelines located at www.apaonline.org/publications/texts/nonsexist.aspx.

consider plagiarism, and any attempt at explaining it in terms of ignorance, differing cultural norms, or the difficulty of writing in English will likely fall on deaf ears. This isn't necessarily because the instructor is insensitive or cruel; it may be because the instructor is not knowledgeable about how hard it is for everyone—especially second language writers—to learn how to paraphrase and credit sources accurately.

Pecorari (2008:12–22) discusses the well-known suggestion that international students have a harder time paraphrasing appropriately because of differing cultural norms (one which I cited in the first edition of this book, in fact), observing that "these culture-based explanations have gained currency in much the same way as urban myths do" (2008:13). That is, she argues that more recent research calls such arguments into question. First, she says that these explanations are simply not supported by the data in recent studies, and second, she shows that the research actually calls into question the very claim that international students plagiarize more.

No matter what your background, all students need to realize that in North American academic culture, *any time* we use an author's ideas and/or words, failure to provide the source (and to use quotation marks where exact wording is copied) is considered the gravest of academic sins.

What Counts as Plagiarism?

The University of Wisconsin Writing Center Writer's Handbook, available at www.wisc.edu/writing/Handbook, includes a very nice section on different types of plagiarism. You might want to check your university's writing center to see if they have anything similar. In addition, there are various books on the topic, such as Harris (2005).

The page from the UW Writing Center first points out the most obvious type of plagiarism: word-for-word plagiarism. Some students think that this only applies to copying whole passages without citation, but in fact borrowing phrases and general sentence structure (not to mention ideas) is just as bad. I've seen many students take sentences from some source and replace key words with synonyms, thinking that this was adequate paraphrasing. It most emphatically is not.

The second type of plagiarism is one that many students—no matter what tradition they were raised in—don't even realize is plagiarism. The UW Writing Center's old handout called this "mosaic plagiarism" (which on their website they have amended to "patchwork plagiarism"). This is when the writer has paid a certain amount of attention to restating central ideas and reworking sentence structure, but still litters the document with bits and pieces that come directly from the original. Although this isn't quite as bad as word-for-word plagiarism, it still counts as plagiarism and must be avoided. I give examples of each type of plagiarism below, which should make this clearer.

Paraphrasing

It takes some practice to learn to write summaries of other people's work that paraphrase appropriately without borrowing too heavily from their prose. The Writer's Handbook I referred to above suggests reading each paragraph (or other convenient unit) of the original as a whole and then stopping to write a summary, instead of jotting down notes while you read. That way you can try to paraphrase the general idea of the original without being overly influenced by the author's particular choice of words.

In this section, I present an original paragraph followed by various attempts at paraphrase.[19] The original is taken from Chomsky (1965:3–4).

Linguistic theory is concerned primarily with an ideal speaker-listener, in a completely homogeneous speech-community, who knows its language perfectly and is unaffected by such grammatically irrelevant conditions as memory limitations, distractions, shifts of attention and interest, and errors (random or characteristic) in applying his knowledge of the language in actual performance. This seems to me to have been the position of the founders of modern general linguistics, and no cogent reason for modifying it has been offered.

Figure 3.1. Original Text

Linguistic theory is concerned with an ideal speaker-hearer, who lives in a completely homogeneous speech community. This person speaks his language perfectly and doesn't notice things like errors, changes in attention and interest, memory limitations, or distractions when using his knowledge of the language in everyday performance. This was the position of the founders of modern general linguistics.

Figure 3.2. Word-for-Word Plagiarism

The paragraph in figure 3.2 would be a completely unacceptable summary of Chomsky's paragraph, in that much of it (the words and phrases which are underlined) is lifted from the original, and used without citation. The writer (okay, it was me) has tried to disguise the plagiarism by moving some phrases around—but please note that this does not count as legitimate paraphrase. In some places this dreadful imaginary student has substituted a synonym (e.g., *changes* for *shifts*), but again, this is not enough. Furthermore, the paragraph follows the

19. This is modeled on the University of Wisconsin Writing Center's handout on quoting and paraphrasing.

original almost exactly in its structure. Now, in some ways the original has been improved upon, in that the excessively long run-on sentence of the original has been broken up into several separate sentences, but nonetheless the structure remains the same, another thing to avoid. Finally, note that our rotten, no-good plagiarizer has not cited Chomsky at all.

> Chomsky (1965:3–4) claims that the founders of modern linguistics believed that linguistics deals with an ideal speaker-listener, and that we should still believe that today. The idealization means that the speaker speaks its language perfectly, without any distractions from performance factors such as mistakes, a faulty memory, changes in attention and interest, etc.

Figure 3.3. Mosaic Plagiarism

The example of mosaic plagiarism in figure 3.3 is certainly better, in that the writer has cited the author, reorganized the structure of the paragraph, and tried to paraphrase most of the content. However, there are still a number of phrases lifted directly from the original without the use of quotation marks, and this is what makes it mosaic plagiarism. I have seen many instances of mosaic plagiarism in student papers, and the students have almost always believed that citing the author makes it acceptable to write in this fashion. It does not.

> Chomsky (1965:3–4) claims that the field of linguistics has long operated with the notion of an "ideal speaker-listener," and says that he sees no reason to reject this position today. The notion of the "ideal speaker-listener" is exactly that—an idealization—that is, someone who has perfect competence in their language, and for whom performance factors play no role.

Figure 3.4. Adequate Paraphrase

In the paragraph in figure 3.4, the author is cited, the structure of the original has not been imitated, and quotation marks are used for the one phrase taken word-for-word from the original. Note that certain words that appeared in the original also appear here—e.g., *position* and *performance*. This is not a problem, though, since they are ordinary words used in very different structures than in the original.

Human Subjects and Informed Consent

If you're working with living, breathing speakers of a language, you have certain ethical obligations to those speakers as well as to their communities and the community of linguists in general. I recommend reading the LSA's Ethics Statement at www.lsadc.org/info/lsa-res.cfm (full disclosure: I worked with the committee that drafted the statement).

You will also need to find out about getting clearance from your university's Human Subjects committee. The process is different at each university, but all American universities by federal law now have guidelines for work with human subjects. At the University of Wisconsin, faculty have to go through the procedure for their graduate students. This involves filling out the appropriate form, and preparing an informed consent document to be given to each of the speakers the investigator works with. The guidelines are very specific, and there is a set of required elements for the form.

The informed consent procedures were developed to protect people from truly invasive experiments. If all you're doing is making an audio recording of a speaker, it may seem silly to you that you are required to go through the process, and you may be tempted to just skip it. Don't! A graduate student in my department narrowly escaped having to redo his entire dissertation study because he failed to get approval. The Human Subjects committee eventually made a grudging exception for him, but not until his dissertation committee had prepared reams of documents explaining what had happened, and put procedures in place to ensure that it would never happen again.

The rules cover all research done with humans, and since it's humans we usually get language data from, we're included in the requirements. At some universities, if you're only doing an audio recording, you can get an "exempt" rating, but generally you still have to go through the process to let them decide that you're exempt. ("Exempt" means that you don't have to do the consent form with each speaker.) If you're doing something more involved, like a phonetics experiment or video recording, the committee will almost certainly require you to get informed consent from your speakers.

Talk to your advisor about how the process works on your campus, and if your advisor doesn't know, find out and educate your advisor. On my campus, there is a web-based training program that you have to work through in order to get certified to do research with human subjects. The training is sort of a pain, since so much of it is not applicable to the kind of research a linguist would do, but it is interesting to learn a bit about the history of human subjects regulations. At any rate, it is extremely important to take care of this, and the penalties for not doing so can be very severe.

Exercise 5: Exploring Library Resources

University libraries have links to databases that provide full text versions of various journals. For example, the University of Wisconsin's library subscribes to JSTOR, a journal archive, from which you can download articles from journals like *Language*. The goal of this exercise is to find out how you can access linguistics journals through your library.

1. Make a list of 10 linguistics journals. You might identify these from the references listed in articles you've read, or by asking others what journals they think are central to your area of interest or to the field in general.

2. Explore your library to find out which ones they provide in print or through electronic access (or both).

    - For each journal available in print, find out whether the journal can be checked out of the library.

    - For each journal available electronically, find out whether you can access the journal from home or only from the library or campus.

    - For each journal that your library does not carry, find out whether the library can get particular articles or journal issues for you through interlibrary loan.

Exercise 6: Argumentation

One way to understand linguistic argumentation is to examine the form that an argument takes in someone else's work. To do this, first find a well-written short article or *Linguistic Inquiry* squib. (If you're working on your own, you might want to ask one of your professors to recommend something short that they think is really well-written and well-argued.) Then take the article apart, breaking it down into its component parts. You can do this exercise on your own, or you can do this with your fellow graduate students and compare your results. The goal is to see explicitly the steps that an author takes in constructing an argument (and for that matter, in constructing an article) so that you can learn to do it yourself.

1. Start by listing the sections that the author divides the article into.

2. Look at each section and trace its structure. You might, for example, find the following kinds of structure in the introduction:

   - A statement of a previous claim or claims
   - The author's claim
   - A roadmap describing how the paper is structured

   Then look at the content sections. You might notice structure along these lines:

   - The data or phenomenon described
   - Theoretical assumptions or background
   - Previous claims about the data or phenomenon
   - Counterexamples
   - The author's solution

   Finally, look at the conclusion. You might find something like this:

   - Restatement of the problem
   - Restatement of the author's solution
   - Comments on further research
   - Theoretical implications

Exercise 7: Human Subjects

1. Find out what the requirements for human subjects are at your college or university. You might get this started by talking to faculty members or more advanced graduate students, or checking your institution's website.

2. Make up a step-by-step flowchart of what you would have to do to be cleared for a hypothetical research project involving human subjects. Figure out what forms have to be filled out (and who has to fill them out), what documents need to be created and submitted, and how long it takes to get approval.

3. Add the research project itself to the flowchart. Would you be required to do anything while the research was in progress and/or once it was completed?

4 Mechanics: How to Write Like a Linguist

It's time now to get down to some of the mechanics of writing a linguistics paper (or article or dissertation). In this chapter, I cover structuring a paper, writing up a quantitative study, using examples, and other aspects of writing the way linguists are expected to write. I will keep returning to the notion of clarity throughout the chapter. There are many ways to enhance the clarity of your presentation, and you should think of the various techniques mentioned here as all working together to produce a maximally comprehensible piece of writing. The obvious reason to strive for clarity is to communicate your ideas efficiently. Keep in mind that most readers of a badly-written paper will conclude that the author can't think clearly either—not a reputation that you want to develop. Luey (2010:11) suggests alternative (also undesirable) reactions: readers might think you just don't know how to write, or worse, that you're trying to hide the fact that you don't have anything to say. So as you work through this chapter, keep coming back to the notion that there are many ways to achieve clarity in your writing.

Structuring a Paper

There are different approaches to structuring a paper, depending on the subfield of linguistics that you're working in. Reports of quantitative research such as experimental and survey work generally follow somewhat different conventions from non-quantitative work in areas like syntax and phonology.[20] The basic idea of structuring a paper with sections that are numbered and titled is standard across all subfields of linguistics, though the structure of a quantitative research paper is more standardized (as discussed later in this chapter). The best way to figure out what format is expected of you is to look carefully at articles describing research which is similar to the type you're doing.

Numbered Sections

Take a look at almost any linguistics journal and you'll notice something about the way the papers are formatted: the sections in the articles (and some books) are numbered and titled. This is illustrated in figure 4.1 below. Section 1 is almost always the introduction (although some people number the introduction

---

20. Quantitative research is research involving measured, counted, and/or statistically analyzed data.

as zero, and others do not number it at all), and the last section is the conclusion. The references do not generally form a numbered section; they are just appended at the end of the paper.

```
1. Introduction
2.
2.1.
2.2.
3.
3.1.
3.1.1.
3.1.2.
3.2.
4. Conclusion
References
```

Figure 4.1. Numbering Sections

Numbering sections is a useful device that makes your steps and logic clear to the reader. The sections make your outline explicit, which can be a big help in understanding a paper. It is also useful to separate sections by an extra blank line, and to put the section number and title in boldface so that the reader can spot it easily. All of these techniques aid the reader in keeping track of the organization of a paper, which can be a tough task when the paper is dense and filled with unfamiliar data and complicated argumentation.

Just as you have to pay attention to choosing a title that accurately reflects your overall topic, the titles of the sections and subsections must also be carefully chosen to reflect the content in question. Make sure that the section title describes all of (and only) what you do in the section. If it doesn't, this may be a signal to you that you need to do some reorganization.

The Introduction

There are two principles that you should follow religiously in the introduction to non-quantitative work: a linguistics paper is not a mystery novel,[21] and your introduction should include a roadmap to your paper. (This is different from the introduction to a quantitative paper, which is discussed later in this chapter.)

---

21. I learned this from Alicja Gorecka, who said that it was a common slogan in the linguistics department at MIT.

A Linguistics Paper Is Not a Mystery Novel

Don't leave the reader in the dark about the solution to the problem until the end of the paper. Say in the introduction what your conclusion is going to be—there is nothing to be gained (and much to be lost) by trying to keep it a secret until the last page. Look over published linguistics papers and note how they do this: often there's an almost formulaic beginning along the lines of "This paper examines X, concluding Y." You don't have to use that precise wording, but you need to get that information across.

Include a Roadmap

The roadmap is a paragraph that tells the reader what to expect in each section. Again, take a look at a selection of published papers, and note how many of them have a paragraph at the end of the introduction that says, "The paper proceeds as follows: in section 2, I consider X. In section 3, I argue that Y . . ." The roadmap is yet another aid to the reader that orients them to the organization of the paper.

The Conclusion

The conclusion supplies a summary of what the paper has accomplished. You may feel like you're being repetitive, but it's still valuable to recap what you've done. Be sure to use different wording than you used to describe your conclusions in the introduction and body of the paper, though, or it *will* sound repetitive.

One mistake I've noticed in the papers of beginning students that should be avoided is putting new information into the conclusion. Don't introduce new facts or new data here. If you feel like you need to discuss something new, go back and put it into the body of the paper. It doesn't belong in the conclusion.

Writing up a Quantitative Study

Some aspects of writing up a quantitative study differ from what has just been described, while others stay the same. One common characteristic is that both types of research are hypothesis-based. The scientific method still applies, as does the concept of repeatedly changing and refining hypotheses until finding one that accounts for all of the data.

Another aspect of quantitative research that does not differ from other kinds of linguistic research is the necessity of doing a thorough bibliographic search before starting your experiment or survey. Just as in any kind of research, it is critically important to know what has gone before you. Review the section on background research in chapter 3, and make yourself a working bibliography.

This section will briefly cover what other authors take entire books to discuss. I strongly suggest that you consult reference works on doing quantitative research after reading this section. Bitchener (2010) is a good resource for writing a quantitative research paper, and Rudestam and Newton (2007) contains several chapters relevant to dissertations involving quantitative research.

Stages in Quantitative Research

Research Design

Plan your project with great attention to detail. Think through each step, and write out a research proposal that lays out everything that you will have to do. Your advisor or committee should then review your proposal—their experience in research design may help you to avoid pitfalls that you could not foresee. There are also many books on experiment and survey design that can guide you through this stage.

Pilot Project

A pilot project is a very small instance of a larger experiment which is done before the large experiment. There are many reasons for doing this; the most obvious and important one is to find flaws in your research design. Even the best research idea can flounder at the point of implementation, which is why it is so important to do the pilot. In addition, the pilot gives you experience at running the experiment or administering the questionnaire, and helps you to become more adept in that role.

Your experimental work as a beginning student may be sufficiently small-scale that a pilot study isn't necessary. Differences between types of experimental work—such as a survey on language attitudes vs. an examination of phonetic data—may also affect whether a pilot is necessary. Check with your advisor about this.

After running your pilot project, analyze your preliminary set of data and revise your research design if necessary. Be sure to get feedback from your advisor at this point, so that they know what your results were. You may have to do major revisions to your design, in which case another round of piloting may be necessary.

The Experiment or Survey

Running the actual study will involve a great deal of planning. Scheduling subjects is the kind of detail that can take much longer than you expect (subjects don't always show up exactly when we want them to, for example). Try to run all of the subjects as close together as possible, without letting too much time elapse. This will minimize the possibility of differences arising across the subject pool, as well as differences in the experimenter's attitude towards the project.

Analyze the Data

If you don't have the necessary statistical background, most universities have some sort of statistical consulting service that you can use. However, if you plan to make quantitative research a mainstay of your future research program, it's time to take those dreaded statistics classes and learn at least the basics for yourself.[22]

Write It Up

This step is the topic of the rest of this chapter.

Writing a Quantitative Research Paper

The sections in a quantitative research paper tend to follow a stricter format than other types of papers. Figure 4.2 shows a standard way of organizing such a paper. Of course, individual papers may deviate somewhat from this format if the topic calls for it, but the standard format can be used as a template for the first draft, with changes made as necessary.

> 1. Introduction
> 2. Method
> 3. Results
> 4. Discussion

Figure 4.2. Sections in a Quantitative Research Paper

Before I turn to discussion of each section, I should note that just as there is flexibility in the sections included, there is flexibility in the content of the sections. For example, some papers combine the results and discussion sections, some mention return rates for questionnaires in the results section instead of the method section, etc. In what appears below, I discuss the usual content of each section, but you should manipulate this to best fit your own study, putting each element where it makes the most sense.

---

22. I found one unexpected problem at this stage when helping a student who was running a phonetics experiment: the only computer lab on campus that had the appropriate statistical software was restricted to students in particular departments—and Linguistics was not one of them. After a few phone calls, though, we got her into the lab. If the faculty in your department don't generally do quantitative research, you may run into problems like this, but your professors should be able to help you find ways around them.

Introduction

In papers reporting experiments or surveys, it is usual to include in the introduction a review of relevant literature. The key word here is "relevant"— don't overdo it! You don't need to mention every single article ever written on the topic, only the most relevant and widely cited.

A much more significant difference between this kind of writing and that described earlier is that the introduction to a quantitative research paper generally does *not* give away the findings. That is, in this type of paper you do save your conclusions until the end—it *is* a mystery novel, though an abstract at the beginning may describe the findings even when the introduction does not. The introduction usually ends with a paragraph or so explaining the perceived need for the study being reported (based on the review of literature), the hypothesis or hypotheses that the author has about the subject, and a brief summary of the study, but without describing the results of the research.

Furthermore, because the basic organization is so standardized, a roadmap isn't necessary. Readers of this type of paper already know the roadmap.

There are a number of ways that authors deviate from the pattern just described, of course. Some have a fairly brief introduction, with one or more sections following that which cover previous literature on the topic and other background information necessary to understand the research. For example, a second language acquisition paper reporting an experiment on a particular syntactic construction might contain a section describing current analyses of that construction.

In addition, some authors provide a separate section with their research questions or hypotheses, or include them at the end of one of the background information sections. Others include them in the *Method* section, discussed next.

Method

This section describes the experiment conducted. Sometimes it's called *The Study*, *The Experiment*, or *Data* instead of *Method,* but all contain a description of the experiment. This description has to be very thorough, describing all relevant aspects of the procedures used, especially those having to do with subjects. Your rationale for constructing the study the way you did should come out in this section as well: why you chose the subjects you chose, why you asked the questions you asked, etc.

The *Method* section should also include discussion of any failures or less than complete results—e.g., subjects who quit the experiment before finishing, replies that had to be discarded, or the return rate for questionnaires that were sent out.

Sometimes authors divide this section up into subsections, e.g., *Subjects, Method,* and *Analysis.* In other cases authors include our next topic, *Results*, as one of these subcategories.

Results

Before presenting your numbers in the results section, you need to discuss the way in which you arrived at those numbers. Describe your statistical methods, including such details as coding procedures, conversion of raw scores to some particular scale, and tests used. Then present the results themselves. This may be simple or it may be complicated, depending on your study. If it is complicated, and different test groups had different outcomes, you may want to divide this section into a number of subsections.

Bem (2004:199) says, "The general rule in reporting your findings is to give the forest first and then the trees." In other words, explain the big picture first and then move to smaller, individual results.

Discussion

This section is the equivalent of the conclusion in a qualitative linguistics research paper (in fact, some authors call it *Discussion and Conclusion*, or even just *Conclusion*). Here you talk about the significance of what you reported in the *Results* section and the conclusions that you can draw from those results. You will need to state explicitly whether your findings support or refute your hypothesis or hypotheses, remembering that negative results count as results in such work.

If others have done similar studies, you should compare your results to those of other studies. How did your results differ, and how does your study resolve some of the questions left open by other researchers?

It is also common to talk about the shortcomings of your own research, but make sure you put a positive spin on them. At the very least you can say that such shortcomings will inform your future research, or point out ways to design better experiments in the future. What you don't want to do here is obsess about your failures, or leave the reader feeling like it was a waste of time to read the paper. A brief, frank statement of problems is all that is called for, and once that's done, you can move on to something else. A typical Something Else is to conclude the paper with suggestions for future research. (Some authors treat this as a separate section, usually placed after the *Discussion* section and called *Implications for Future Research*, or something along those lines.)

Another element that often appears in the *Discussion* section, at least for second language acquisition papers, is some mention of the pedagogical implications of the research. (And you won't be surprised to learn that some writers make this a separate section too.)

Finally, if a survey or questionnaire was administered, it should be included in an appendix at the end of the paper unless it's too long to be reasonably included.

Using Examples, Presenting Data

Linguists' papers are often very data-heavy. It is absolutely imperative that you choose relevant examples, lay them out clearly, and explain their relevance to your claim or hypothesis. This section discusses choosing the right example, example format, and the incorporation of examples into the text of your paper.[23]

Choosing the Right Example

It's fairly easy to choose an example that illustrates the point you want to make. Make sure, though, that your example illustrates *only* the point that you want to make. A common beginner's mistake is to use an example that includes the relevant phenomenon, but includes so much else that clarity is lost. As an example, suppose I'm writing a paper on topicalization in some language. When it comes time to exemplify the construction I'm writing about, if my examples show topicalization but are also, say, passive, it might be hard for my readers to figure out what I'm getting at. Furthermore, my readers might think that the fact that the sentences are passive has some relevance that I've missed, which would undermine the claim that I'm making. So use the simplest possible example of your phenomenon, and as you illustrate different aspects of it, vary only one thing at a time.

Formatting Examples

Examples should be numbered consecutively from the beginning to the end of the paper. The numbers should not restart with each section, although in a dissertation it is common to restart them with each chapter. Example numbers should appear at the left margin of the page, rather than indented like a paragraph.[24] Consider the following example of an example:

(1) This is an example of an example

If you have several closely-related examples to present, you can group them together under one number, using letters to distinguish them, as in:

(2) a.   This is one version of an example
     b.   This is another version of an example

---

23. I won't talk here about the conventions for presenting conversational data. These are complicated and extremely precise; consult an expert on this.

24. Some journals have different preferred styles, but this is the most common way and, in my opinion, the clearest way.

The numbers and letters allow you to refer to the examples in the text. For the example itself, it doesn't really matter whether you put a period after your number or put parentheses around it. But when referring to an example in the text it's best to put parentheses around the number, because it stands out better that way and it's what readers in the field expect. Notice how much easier on the eye it is when I say that (1) shows something very important, as opposed to saying that 1. shows something important.

Examples in an unfamiliar language need to be translated, and in most cases, glossed. (The exception, of course, is if you're giving single morphemes or words, in which case the gloss would be the same as the translation.) The gloss line gives a translation of each morpheme and is sandwiched between the data and the full translation. Consider (3), an example from Chalcatongo Mixtec:[25]

(3) xížaa=ðe šinì žuku
    be.located=3M head mountain
    'He is at the top of the mountain'
    (Brugman 1983:239)

In (3), the first line is the data line, the second is the gloss line, and the third is the translation. Notice, however, that it's a little hard to read, the way that I've presented it. This is because I didn't line up the words. Examples are easier to follow with each word lined up, as in (4):

(4) xížaa=ðe   šinì žuku
    be.located=3M head mountain
    'He is at the top of the mountain'

Figuring out which word in the data line corresponds to which word in the gloss line is not such a big deal for a simple sentence like this one, but you can imagine how difficult it would be to work through a much longer, more complicated sentence if the words were not lined up.

If the language is fairly agglutinating—that is, if the boundaries between the morphemes are clear—you can just provide the three lines described above. But if there's a lot of fusion in the data—if the boundaries between morphemes are blurred—you may need to add another line which provides the underlying form of the utterance, as in the following Karuk example:

(5) víri hû:t ikupe:θvásipre:he:š
    víri hû:t ʔi-   kupa- ʔí:θva-sipriv-ahi   -aviš
    so   how 2SG>3PL(POS)-MODAL-pack -up   -MODAL-FUT
    'How would you pack them?'

---

25. The equals sign separates a clitic from its host. A hyphen could also be used.

In (5), notice that I haven't just lined up the words; I've lined up the morphemes with their glosses. This is because the last word of the example is so long and complicated that not doing so would make it quite hard for the reader to figure out which Karuk morpheme goes with which gloss.

One exception to the above is when the specific morphemic composition of the words doesn't matter for the point you're trying to get across. So if all I was trying to illustrate was the use of the initial particle in the Karuk example just given, I might present it as in (6a) or even as in (6b):

(6) a. víri hû:t ikupe:θvásipre:he:š
         so how 2SG>3PL(POS).MODAL.pack.up.MODAL.FUT
         'How would you pack them?'

     b. víri hû:t ikupe:θvásipre:he:š
         so how you would pack them
         'How would you pack them?'

There are a number of other conventions in example presentation, but there is also a fair bit of variation across linguists and across journal style sheets. I'll list some of the most common conventions here, but be forewarned that you will undoubtedly come across other ways of doing this.

Conventions in Example Presentation

- Separate affixes from stems and other affixes by using hyphens, in both the data line and the gloss line.

- Use either hyphens or equals signs to separate clitics from their hosts.

- If it takes more than one English word to translate a single morpheme in the data, separate those English words with periods (as in 'be.located' in (4)). A plus sign is sometimes used for this purpose, although it's less standard.

- Put glosses of grammatical morphemes into a font which contrasts in some way with the font used for glosses which translate lexical morphemes. In the examples above, I've used small capitals for the grammatical morphemes. Others capitalize the entire word or just the first letter of the gloss.

- Put the free translation of the example into single quotes, or use no quotes at all. Double quotes are generally not used.

- If your examples come from some published source, somewhere in your paper say where they are taken from. You might be able to state it just once, perhaps in a footnote, if all examples come from the same source. But if the examples are drawn from various sources, you should provide the source of each example as it is given. Note that I did this for example (3).

- Don't break your examples across pages. For example, don't allow the data line and the gloss line to appear at the bottom of one page and the translation at the top of the next. This is fine for the drafts you write for your own purposes, but as soon as you format a draft to show to a professor or fellow student, or to submit to a journal or other publication, put in a hard page break so that the entire example appears together. It is extremely difficult to process examples when you have to keep flipping pages back and forth.

Incorporating Examples into the Text

Examples can't just float in a text with nothing to anchor them to that text. They need to be introduced, and they need to be discussed.

There are several formulaic ways to introduce examples. You've just seen a few of them above (e.g., "Consider the following . . . ," "as in," and "as in (4)"), and a longer list appears below. In addition, you can do something less formulaic, such as using a colon at the end of the sentence immediately before the example.

Example Introductions

- as shown in (12):
- as (12) illustrates:
- for example:
- as in:
- as in the following examples:
- Consider (12):
- Consider the following examples:
- See (12)–(14):
- I found only one example of this:
- Of the languages considered, Menominee has the most complex rules of stress assignment:
- Forms with glottalized stops include:
- The negative particle that is used with negative order is *kan*, as illustrated in (12)–(14).
- The examples in (12)–(14) provide evidence for this argument.
- An example of each is given below.

Try to mix and match your example introductions. It can get very repetitive if you do it the same way each time.

Once you've introduced the example, your work is only half over. You still need to discuss the example. Typically, the order is introduction–example–discussion, although this can vary. In the discussion, you need to do two things: you need to explain what's going on in the example, and you need to explain its significance to your claim or to the topic under discussion.

Consider the following excerpt from a paper that I coauthored with Joseph Salmons (Macaulay and Salmons 1995):

Taking as our example the case of Ayutla Mixtec (as described in Pankratz and Pike 1967), we find couplets with the forms shown in (12). In these examples, tone is marked as follows: 1 – high, 2 – mid, 3 – low. Stress is marked by acute accent.

(12) Ayutla Mixtec
    a. CV?CV: yá³?vi³ 'market'
    b. CVCV?:   ná²ma³? 'soap'
    c. CV?CV?:   ka³?ví¹? 'younger brother'

It is the second example (*ná²ma³?* 'soap') which shows that glottalization does not correlate with stress in Ayutla Mixtec, since the second syllable is glottalized but not stressed. An analysis which accounts for the distributional patterns of glottalization by restricting it to stressed syllables will not be able to account for glottalization in Ayutla Mixtec.

Notice in this excerpt that we introduce our example ("we find couplets with the forms shown in (12)"), then we give the example, then we explain the feature of the second of the three examples that makes our point ("glottalization does not correlate with stress in Ayutla Mixtec"), and finally we explain why the example is important (because it counterexemplifies a claim that another author had made).

Tables and Figures

If you have tables and figures in your work, you should incorporate these where they are mentioned in the text. Examples are often unlabeled, but each table and figure should have a number and title above or below it. Tables and figures should be numbered separately from examples and from each other, so you may have an example (1), a table 1, and a figure 1 in a single work.

Numerical data can be presented in many different sorts of tables, charts, and graphs. When choosing how to present numerical data, choose a form that is easy for the reader to understand and focuses the reader on the point you want to make. Visual materials can be an easy way to see patterns or differences, but they can also be misleading or distracting.

You may think that your table or figure makes an obvious point, but just as with examples, you have to state that point explicitly in your text. As you discuss the data you present in a table or figure, make sure to repeat the relevant data in the text itself. For example, you might say, "As table 1 shows, 22.3% of respondents said that . . ." Do not force your readers to search for numbers in a table while they are reading your text.

Citing Linguistic Data

When citing a linguistic form in your text, italicize it and provide a gloss. For example, if I wanted to talk about the Menominee word *pōsōh* 'hello,' that's how I would do it. The form itself is in italics, the gloss is in single quotes, and there is no punctuation separating the two.

Be very careful to distinguish between use and mention: the above was an example of mention. That is, I was talking about a form, not using it. When you use something in a foreign language, don't italicize it. For example, I might write, "This is an ad hoc argument." In that quote, I haven't italicized *ad hoc* because I'm using, not mentioning it.[26]

Citations and References

Every work you cite in the text of your paper must be listed in the references section at the end of the paper. The references section is not a general bibliography, though, so do not include references there that you don't cite in the paper. If there are important works on your topic that you want to list in the references section, you must find a way to cite them in the text as well. This can be as simple as saying, "Several other authors have also discussed this phenomenon (Citation 1, Citation 2, Citation 3)," but it's generally more helpful to your readers if you provide at least a hint of what each author has actually said in their work.

Linguistics doesn't have a single universally accepted style sheet the way some other fields such as psychology and literary studies do. However, the Committee of Editors of Linguistics Journals (CELxJ; www.celxj.org) has developed a unified style sheet for references. Many linguistics journals have adopted it, and it's the best default style for you to adopt too.

It's vitally important that your citations and references be complete and accurate. Check that journal articles include volume numbers and page ranges, that papers published in books include the book title and publisher, and that year and author names are accurate. Mistakes and incomplete information can make it difficult or impossible for your readers to find the works that you cite. It's also easy to forget that you have added or removed citations in a new draft, so always do a final check on your citations and references section before you send out a manuscript.

There are numerous styles for citing other authors' works within the text. I have found that most students have been taught MLA style, which is almost never used in linguistics. Instead, the most common style of citation is to use

---

26. I did italicize it in that last sentence. Why? Think about it.

the author's last name with the year of publication in parentheses; e.g., Lamott (1994). One exception to this is when the entire citation is inside parentheses, in which case you should omit the parentheses around the date; e.g., (see Lamott 1994). If you're citing a particular page or pages in the work, put the page number(s) immediately after the year separated by a colon and no spaces; e.g., Lamott (1994:18–19). For a work with two authors, list both; e.g., Glatthorn and Joyner (2005). For a work with more than two authors, list the first author followed by "et al." in citations (and don't leave out that period after "al."), but don't use "et al." in the references section—you must list all authors there. If you cite more than one work by the same author published in the same year, use lowercase letters after the year in both the citation and the references section (e.g., 1981a, 1981b) to differentiate the works.[27]

Citing Online Materials

There is tremendous variation in how online materials are cited and formatted in references sections. Online materials frequently move or disappear, so keep a copy for yourself of anything you think you may want to cite later along with its original URL and the date you accessed it. When you want to include an online reference in your work, provide the title and author as well as the URL to make it easier for your readers to find the material themselves or verify whether what they have found is what you referenced. Most authors also include a note after the URL saying when they accessed the site, along the lines of "last accessed 10/12/2010."

If you are looking for online material that is no longer at its cited location, you have several options. You can search for the title and author, for key words, or for quotes from the work. You can check the exact URL at the Internet Archive's Wayback Machine (www.archive.org) to see if a copy was saved there. And finally, you can contact the author.

Citation Managers

Citation managers are programs that help you create and format a list of references—both the kind you put together for your own use, and the kind you put into your paper. There are several available; popular ones include RefWorks, EndNote, ProCite, Reference Manager, Papers, and Zotero. Your university library probably has information on citation managers on its website, and may

---

27. Conventions on citations vary among academic fields, so, for example, a paper on computational linguistics that is intended for a computer science audience should use the citation conventions of computer science. Style sheets for different journals and different publishers vary as well, so you will see some exceptions to these rules, such as in the use of parentheses around the year.

supply one or more for your use. Wikipedia provides a comparison of many features of different citation managers at en.wikipedia.org/wiki/Comparison_of_ reference_management_software.

These programs make creating your own database of relevant references much, much easier. They can automatically retrieve bibliographical information from citation databases (so that you don't have to do all that cutting and pasting), format references in a given style, and insert references into your paper's references section automatically. These are extremely useful programs, and it is well worth the initial investment of effort it takes to learn to use one.

Footnotes

A student once proudly told me that he never used footnotes because he believed that if it wasn't worth saying in the text, it wasn't worth saying. This may sound like a noble position, but it misses the point. Footnotes are places to put asides that would otherwise clutter up the flow of your text. The writing style in linguistics is not like that found in a law review article, where many pages consist of more footnote text than main text, but linguists do typically use a fair number of footnotes.

I've noticed that many beginning writers have a hard time knowing when something is worth putting in a footnote, when it should go in the text, and when the comment should simply not be made. I don't have any simple formula to suggest, but the closest I can come is to say that a footnote should be relevant (for example, answering a possible objection, or adding some relevant but tangential information) but not central to the topic under discussion.

There are two specific types of footnote that usually appear in a linguistics article: the first footnote and the abbreviations footnote.

First Footnote

The first footnote usually comes at the end of the title (although the style sheets of journals vary on where exactly it is placed). This is a conventional foot-note that contains acknowledgments and other information such as background on the language (when that is not important enough to the topic to go in the body of the paper), sources of funding for the research, etc. Here's (part of) the first footnote to a paper I wrote:

> 1. Mixtec is an Otomanguean language spoken in south-central Mexico by approximately 320,000 people . . . It is made up of a large number of mutually unintelligible varieties, called "dialects" by Mixtecanists. Chalcatongo Mixtec is an Alta dialect spoken by a few thousand people. I would like to thank [names here] for their help and comments on this paper. (Macaulay 1993:73)

Make sure that you remember to thank *all* the people who read your paper, as well as anyone who discussed it with you in any significant way. (It's better to be safe than sorry here.) The example above doesn't do this, but it is very common for authors to add a disclaimer after the acknowledgment such as: "Any errors are my own responsibility," or "Needless to say, none of the above are responsible for the content of this paper."

Abbreviations Footnote

If you're presenting data in the traditional three-line or four-line format, you will no doubt use abbreviations in your glosses. It is imperative that you include a list of what those abbreviations stand for. The place to list the abbreviations is either in a separate footnote that is placed right before the first example that uses an abbreviation or in the first footnote along with the acknowledgments. Here is a shortened version of the abbreviations footnote that I had in the paper cited above:

> 3. Abbreviations used in this paper are as follow: 1, 2, 3 — 1st, 2nd, 3rd persons, AN—animate, COP—copula, CP—completive, F—feminine, TEMP—temporal. High tone is marked with acute accent, mid tone is unmarked, and low tone is marked with grave accent.

Details Matter

I'm sure it's obvious that you should always present your arguments and data as clearly as possible. There are, however, certain housekeeping issues that students often overlook. Following the tips in this section will allow your professors and other readers to focus on your ideas rather than on unimportant details.

Spellcheck and Proofread

Always, always spellcheck and proofread your paper before turning it in or sending it out. I use a handout in my writing class that consists of two gigantic words (and one small one): "SPELLCHECK and PROOFREAD," and I tell the students to tape this to the wall above their computers. With the spellcheckers provided in all word processors there is no excuse for most typos. At the same time, you do have to remember that even the best spellchecker won't pick it up if you accidentally type the wrong word (say, *form* when you mean *from*). This is why you also have to proofread your papers carefully.

Why bother? It's simple: the reader will be distracted if there are typos and other errors in your paper. Or worse, they may be utterly bewildered if there are cut-and-paste errors where you think you've done some revision but have only partially completed it. Your goal is to have the reader concentrate on the content of your paper, not its form.

Identify Your Work

When you turn in a paper, be sure to put the following on the first page: your name, the date, the title of your paper, and the class for which you wrote it (unless it wasn't written for a specific class).[28] The paper can start on the same page as the title—that is, a separate cover page is not necessary unless you're submitting to a journal that requires it in its style sheet.

Page Numbers

Provide page numbers—if I drop the paper and it scatters all over the floor, this will help me put it back together again. Besides, I like to know how much I have to read.

Font Size, Margins, and Spacing

Be kind to your poor old professors' eyes: use a 12-point font. Also use 1-inch margins and double-space your paper to provide plenty of room for comments.

Danger: Excessive Terminology and Thesaurus Style

There are two related problems that have to do with the lexical items writers choose: the overuse of terminology and what I have christened "thesaurus style."

Beginning writers often think it makes them sound more professional to lard their prose with lots of technical terms. Try to limit your use of technical terms to those situations where they are really needed and appropriate. As I've said before, clarity is valued above obfuscation in this field, and too many superfluous technical terms can obscure what you're trying to say.

When are such terms really needed? A friend in the field of literary criticism once complained to me that she was criticized for using too much "jargon," but pointed out that jargon develops for a reason: to express shared ideas in a field precisely and unambiguously. She was right—there is a time and place for the use of technical terms. The key is to avoid overuse.

One way to gauge this is to think about your audience. If you're writing a paper for a journal that publishes in a very specific area, you may be able to use very technical terms, and to do so without defining them. But for a more general

---

28. One of the reasons I like to have the date on a student paper is that then I can glance at it and know if I'm shamefully overdue in returning comments. I don't usually encourage guilt-tripping your professors, but this is a nice subtle technique.

audience, you might want to be more careful about overuse, and to provide more definitions when you do use terms that are particular to your area or theory. For example, if you were writing a paper in the framework of Optimality Theory for a journal devoted exclusively to phonology, you probably wouldn't have to define terms like "correspondence constraint" or abbreviations like "RED." But if you were trying to get such a paper published in a journal of general linguistics, it might behoove you to explain your terms.[29]

A related problem is one for which we can place the blame squarely on the shoulders of the English teachers of the world. As Nida (1946:243) points out, we are taught by such teachers to avoid repetition of the same words and structures in our writing, and to search out alternative ways of saying things when we must repeat a thought or point. This leads to hideous results for inexperienced writers of linguistics papers: what the thesaurus lists as synonyms are not, of course, true synonyms, and the result can be imprecision or worse.

Furthermore, thesaurus style sounds downright silly in a scientific (or even just scholarly) context. Becker (2007:27) describes trying to get a student to replace the phrase *could afford not to have to be concerned with* with *needn't worry about*, and says that her reason for resisting his suggestion was that it sounded "classier" her way. He (and the student) eventually concluded that many of us assume that (a) smart people use big words and long sentences, and (b) if we can't understand somebody, they must be smarter than us. This leads us to believe that scholarly writing has to have lots of big words and long sentences in it to be impressive, and to convince the reader that the writer really knows what they are talking about.

I've seen students attempt classy writing by using, for example, *aver* instead of *say*, *opine* instead of *claim*, or *penned* instead of *wrote*. One student wrote "As witnessed by (2):" when introducing an example. Another common example of this is to use *state* instead of *say*. (Note that *state* has an implication of authority, which I think is why students like to use it. But this implication, along with the presumption that what is stated is fact, is inappropriate when describing an author's claims or arguments.) If you make your mantra "more straightforward is better" you will avoid this tendency and be a better writer as a result.

---

29. Nida (1946:240–243) has a short section devoted to the subject of terminology. Although it was written over a half century ago, much of the advice has stood the test of time and I recommend looking at his suggestions. They are, of course, aimed at an audience of structuralists, and for that matter are highly specific, but they contain some good advice nonetheless.

My Personal Top Ten Least Favorite Writing Habits

The following is a list of ten recurring problems I've noted in linguistics graduate students' writing over the years. Where relevant I've given some examples taken from actual student papers and other sources (although I've modified them so that they are not recognizable), along with a suggested rewording. Of course, when I give a better version of something, it's not the *only* possible alternative. There are always many alternatives available.

1. Excessive Verbiage

Try to streamline your prose.

Instead of: This book is written to provide a general account of . . .
    Use: This book provides a general account of . . .

Instead of: The purpose of this study is to provide an analysis of . . .
    Use: This study provides an analysis of . . .

Instead of: I wish to call attention to the fact that X
    Use: X

Instead of: I would like to point out that X
    Use: Note that X
      or X

Instead of: What I mean by X is Y
    Use: X is defined as Y
      or I define X as Y
      or X is Y

2. Hedging

Hedges are a way of beating around the bush, and are usually intended to ward off potential criticism. Although it is very tempting to use them, they undermine your argument and claims.

Instead of: In this paper, I will try to show that X
    Use: In this paper, I show that X

Instead of: This paper attempts to solve this problem by . . .
    Use: This paper solves the problem by . . .

Instead of: Goldsmith (1999) seems to claim that X
    Use: Goldsmith (1999) claims that X

Instead of: I think this shows X
    Use: This shows X

3. Describing the Process of Discovery

Hockett (1966:67), citing Bloomfield, has a nice line on this: "Bloomfield used to say 'don't take your guests in the kitchen.'" In other words, your readers do not need to know every step you took to arrive at your results. Some examples follow:

> *Instead of:*   As I discovered in a study I did on X . . .
>   *Use:*   I have found Y
>   *or* My study of X shows that Y

> *Instead of:*   Now I would like to find out if the coda gets a mora during syllabification
>   *Use:*   I consider next whether the coda gets a mora during syllabification
>   *or* Does the coda get a mora during syllabification?
>   *or* This example shows that the coda gets/does not get a mora during syllabification

4. Using Contractions

Don't do it.[30]

5. Citing Textbooks

Textbooks are not where an author lays out his or her own research, but instead provide a summary of an area of research.[31] You need to show that you're familiar with the primary literature on a topic, so you need to cite that rather than a textbook on the subject.

6. Using Commas as Transitions

> *Instead of:*   Then restart your browser, it will solve most problems.
>   *Use:*   Then restart your browser. This will solve most problems.
>   *or* Then restart your browser; this will solve most problems.
>   *or* Then restart your browser—this will solve most problems.

---

30. The attentive reader will have noticed that I've been using contractions throughout this book. That's because I made a conscious decision to write this book in a colloquial style rather than a scholarly style. Contractions are not appropriate for scholarly writing, however.

31. Even when a textbook does reflect the author's own work, that work has been published elsewhere earlier.

7. *Misusing* refer *and* referent

This one drives me especially crazy because linguists of all people should know how to use these terms!

Instead of:	Subjacency refers to the fact that
Use:	Subjacency is . . .
	or 'Subjacency' means . . .

Instead of:	Originally borrowed words for animals change over time, and become the primary referents for the animals in many of these languages
Use:	Originally borrowed words for animals change over time, and become the primary terms for the animals in many of these languages

8. *Afterthoughts*

Don't just add some random item at the end of your nicely constructed paragraph, e.g.:

> Smith (2001) observes that the readings of example (1) are dependent on context. (2) indicates that Pat's actions occurred in the remote past, (3) that the action does not continue into the present, and (4) that the action has been completed by the time of the speech act. The interpretation of (2) and (3) involves the past tense, while that of (4) makes use of perfective aspect. All of the sentences specify that the action occurred in the past. Jones (1942) says this language does not have a progressive.

9. *Splitting Sentences across Examples*

Instead of:
. . . whether the language requires pronominal subjects, as in English:
 (1) a. I walk b. *Walk
or whether it does not, as in Spanish:
 (2) a. Yo camino b. Camino

Use:
. . . whether the language requires pronominal subjects, as in English (1), or whether it does not, as in Spanish (2):
 (1) a. I walk b. *Walk
 (2) a. Yo camino b. Camino

10. *Using* assume

Students often describe the work of another author using the word *assume*. If the article or book got published, I assure you that the author did not assume any significant point in their research: they may have hypothesized it, argued for it, or claimed it, but they surely did not assume it. Of course, there are a few exceptions to this. For example, an author may want to make use of the position of another author. In such a case, it is appropriate to write, e.g., *For the purposes of this paper, I assume the analysis presented in Smith (1992)*. Or for a relatively minor point, an author might make a suggestion about a solution; e.g., *I assume that this is due to X, but I leave verification to future research.*

Likewise, make sure *you* don't make assumptions—if you write something like *I assume that [w] is a phoneme in this language*, your reader will think, *but how do they know it's a phoneme?* Argue for a position; never assume one.

Exercise 8: Paper Structure and Example Formatting

1. Take a linguistics article and copy out the section numbers and headings. When you're done, look and see what story they tell. Think through the way that the author organized the article, and how the author brings you along through the process of developing and laying out the article's ideas.

2. Choose three linguistics papers that you've read, and answer the questions below about each paper.

   Structure and Content

   a. Does the author say in the introduction what the paper is about and what conclusions he or she draws, or is it written like a mystery novel?

   b. Is there new information in the conclusion?

   c. What elements does the first footnote contain?

   d. Is there a separate abbreviations footnote?

   Examples

   e. If the examples are not from well-known languages, are they shown in three-line or four-line example format (or something else)?

   f. How are words and/or morphemes lined up? Do you find them easy to read?

   g. Look back at the list of example conventions on pages 60–61 and note what conventions the author follows.

   h. What example introductions does the author use? Make a list of all of them.

3. Compare your results for the three articles and note what kinds of similarities and differences you find. Remember that you may get different results depending on what area of linguistics the papers cover.

Exercise 9: Your Least Favorite Writing Habit

Okay, I got to list my top ten least favorite writing habits. Now it's your turn.

1. Come up with at least one additional writing habit that you consider unforgiveable or at least stylistically displeasing. This could be something you used to do or something you've found in an article or book. If it occurred in a published work, include a complete reference to that work.

2. Propose a way to correct the problem—or even several ways.

3. If you're doing this for a class, make a combined list of everyone's contributions and distribute the list to everyone in the class. Send a copy of the list to me as well (mmacaula@wisc.edu).

5 The Process of Writing

In this chapter I discuss strategies that can help make the writing process a bit easier. Various problems such as writer's block beset most of us at one point or another, but finding the approach that works best for you will make the time you put into writing more productive and satisfying. This will become more and more important as you progress in graduate school.

Anne Lamott on Writing as a Job

"Do it every day for a while," my father kept saying. "Do it as you would do scales on the piano. Do it by prearrangement with yourself. Do it as a debt of honor. And make a commitment to finishing things." (Lamott 1994:xxii)

A Place to Work

All writing guides emphasize the importance of finding a place that you feel comfortable working in. Not wanting to buck the trend, I too advise my students to find such a place. A few departments are lucky enough to have space for graduate student offices, but most don't. (In my department we're lucky to have an office for our Teaching Assistants.) Unless you live alone, it can be hard to carve out a corner at home where you can work quietly, without interruption. You will have to negotiate with your family or roommates for the space and for the quiet. Make sure this is explicitly negotiated so that you don't find yourself tearing out your hair and shrieking at people without warning.

If this just doesn't work out, or if you're the type who doesn't work well at home (there are, after all, all those distractions in the form of the TV, the refrigerator, and that bathroom that needs to be cleaned), try a library carrel. Most graduate libraries have little cell-like spaces that you can reserve for a semester or longer. Depending on whether the doors lock and whether you are the sole occupant, you may be able to leave your books and other materials there. Carrels work for some people, but others find them oppressive. Give one a try, though, if you're having trouble getting work done at home.

Structure

One problem in getting writing (and indeed, any work) done is a lack of structure. Phillips and Pugh (2010:2) characterize this aspect of graduate school with the slogan "under your own management." Some people are good self-starters, but many of us need some sort of external structure in order to get things done. One way to impose structure is to have some sort of writing group (see below). Another is to simply ask your advisor to help you out by establishing deadlines for your work (or stages of your work). This becomes especially important at the dissertation-writing stage, and this is discussed further in chapter 8. The key here is to make sure you recognize that you need structure, and to find a way to create it.[32]

Getting Started

Getting started can be extremely difficult. This is the point at which I usually suffer my worst avoidance. But I'll let you in on a secret: it took me years to figure this out, but I finally realized that the days or weeks that I spend fretting about getting started are actually part of the process. I've written enough papers now to recognize what I'm doing, and usually I just let myself do it. You, however, might not have the luxury of wasting several weeks (sometimes I don't either, of course), so if you find yourself doing this, make yourself take some steps to get started. Like I said above, the key is to recognize what you're doing.

Becker (2007:2–3) points out that we all have our own little writing quirks. Do you have to arrange your desk just so? Does it have to be night-time? Do you have to clean the house before you can write? He describes getting people in his writing class to fess up to the rituals that they have, and some of the things that come out are pretty hilarious. I've tried it in my classes too, and the best response I got was from a student who said that he had to take a shower before he could write. He said it made him think better if his brain was clean.

Becker's analysis of this kind of behavior is that we turn to ritual precisely when we fear that we lack control over something. Lining up your pencils or taking a ritual shower gives you a feeling of control, thereby convincing you that the writing will go well. (Of course, the longer the ritual takes, the better, since that also postpones the moment when you actually have to get started.) Becker makes a good point here: wouldn't it be better just to take control over your writing?

---

32. Eventually, of course, you will have to wean yourself off of the people who create structure for you (especially if you go on to get an academic job), but these suggestions can help if you're really stuck. Chapter 8 discusses ways for you to impose structure on yourself.

In fact, once I read Becker's description of this, I realized that over the years, as writing has become easier for me, I have lost the rituals that I had in graduate school. Aside from some obligatory fretting, I can now generally just sit down and write. I hope that you too will experience over time a lessening of the difficulties that writing can pose, and that some of the approaches suggested in this chapter help you to get control over the process.

Outlining

Do you remember learning in school how to make an outline? I do. We were drilled on the proper symbols to use at each level (Roman numerals here, capital letters there, etc.), and made to feel that great calamity would befall us if we got it wrong. What I took away from this training was a very rigid concept of the outline and a corresponding aversion to ever making or using an outline.

As a graduate student, I developed my own way of organizing my thoughts when I was writing, and it wasn't until much later that I realized that what I was doing was outlining—but without the rigid approach I had been taught in school.

If you like doing formal outlines, that's great—do it that way. But if you're not comfortable with them, you might try the method I use (demonstrated below). Either way, you need to do something that will force you to organize your thoughts. Don't just start writing. What will result is a stream-of-consciousness mess, and it will take you longer to untangle that than it would if you had made some sort of outline in the first place.[33]

Following then, is a mini-demonstration of how I start writing something. In this case, it was a short document for the College of Letters and Science at the UW, for an exercise they called "Establishing Our Focus." (This is the fun kind of stuff you get to do when you're a department chair.) Our Dean wanted to establish a limited number of priorities that would be used for deciding on faculty hirings through a special program initiated by the Chancellor. This particular submission argued for a focus on language in general, and more specifically for American Indian languages.

As I said, I have my own peculiar way of "outlining": First I just write down everything I can think of that I want to say, in no particular order. (I use a lot of abbreviations, too, because I try to get these things written down fast before I forget anything.) The list I made up for this particular exercise is illustrated in figure 5.1.

---

33. As you will see below, I actually do advocate a version of the stream-of-consciousness approach (called the "spew draft"), but you still need an outline to organize it.

Establishing Our Focus: American Indian Languages at the UW

lg as a focus for L&S
diversity issues
Am Ind lgs' contribution to study of lg in gen'l
dire situation of Am Ind lgs
special situation in WI
WI idea
need rep's of other 2 lg fam's

Figure 5.1. First Attempt at an Outline

Then I look over the list I've made, and start trying to put it into some kind of logical order, indenting where I think one thing fits under another. (I've unabbreviated in figure 5.2 just so you can tell what I meant; I don't usually do that for my own purposes.)

Establishing Our Focus: American Indian Languages at the UW

language as a focus for Letters and Science
    this document about American Indian languages
several reasons why important
    American Indian languages' contribution to study
    of language in general
        give example?
    dire situation of American Indian languages
    special situation in Wisconsin
        "Wisconsin idea"
        need representatives of other 2 language families
        history of study here?
    diversity issues
conclusion

Figure 5.2. Second Attempt at an Outline

Then I start writing, keeping in mind that one never has to write from beginning to end. The next section talks about approaching writing in small chunks, but there's no rule anywhere that says that you have to start with the first item on the outline. I generally just take my sketchy outline and start filling things in where I feel like it. As I write, I think of things that I left out of the outline, and I go back and put those in so that I don't forget them. This also helps me keep an eye on the organization, so that the new points I come up with get incorporated into the right spot. Figure 5.3 shows the final version of the outline for this short document that I wrote.

Establishing Our Focus: American Indian Languages at the UW

language as a focus for Letters and Science
    this document re American Indian languages
    background: special situation in Wisconsin
several reasons why important
    American Indian languages' contribution to study
    of language in general (theoretical and sociolinguistic)
        give example
    diversity issues
        importance of teaching American Indian languages
    dire situation of American Indian languages
    outreach to the community
        "Wisconsin idea"
        need representatives of other 2 languge families here at UW
conclusion
    (mention hire proposal)

Figure 5.3. Outline Developed while Writing

Now, I picked a non-research document to illustrate the notion of evolving outlines just to make my explanation simpler. Naturally, for a research paper you have to intersperse the organization and outlining parts with the data analysis parts, and it is a much more involved process.

The crucial point to remember, though, is that outlines are not cast in stone. They are intended to be flexible—it's *good* to go back and reconsider things, to reorganize, and to make changes. That means that you're developing your ideas, and it's natural that ideas will change as they develop.

The "Bird by Bird" Method

When I teach my writing course, I always assign Anne Lamott's 1994 book, *Bird by Bird*. Although it's a book on fiction writing, I find that almost everything in it is useful for graduate students learning to do scholarly writing. It may be that the chapters on developing your characters' personalities aren't the most relevant to a linguistics paper (in fact, I don't assign those chapters), but the general ideas are incredibly helpful and her own writing is beautiful. While it's very easy for a book on writing to get dry and tedious, Lamott's book is a joy to read. I highly recommend it.

The title of the book comes from a scene out of her childhood. Her brother had to write a paper on birds, which he was starting the night before it was due. Lamott says that he was, understandably, "immobilized by the hugeness of the task ahead." She continues, "Then my father sat down beside him, put his arm around my brother's shoulder, and said 'Bird by bird, buddy. Just take it bird by bird'" (1994:18–19).

The point is that an overwhelmingly large task can only be accomplished in small stages. The only way to get a paper or a dissertation written is to break it into smaller pieces, and work on those pieces one at a time. Part of the trick is to fool yourself into thinking that the small chunk is all you have to do, because as soon as you let yourself think about the project as a whole, that overwhelmed feeling will come rushing right back at you.

There are all sorts of little tricks you can play on yourself to make the bird by bird method work. Keep a list of the pieces of your project (the sections or other chunks that you break it up into) and check them off as they get written. When I was writing my dissertation, I started a binder, and I would print out the sections that I wrote as they were finished, and put them into the binder. That way when I was feeling like I would never get the thing done, I could look at the binder and see how much I had already accomplished. I remember riffling through the pages over and over, thinking, "Okay, there's a lot here, I've gotten a lot done already, just keep going." I found it very comforting to be able to do that. Concentrate on what you've already done instead of what's left to do, and then just keep plugging away at it, bird by bird.

The Nike Method

Nike has a slogan, "Just do it." I suggest that as a mantra for my students when they are having trouble getting started. A very common reason for writing avoidance is the fear that what one writes will not be any good. And since the stuff that most of us write when we first sit down at the desk usually *isn't* very good, it's easy to use this as evidence that we're just never going to be able to do it well, or even at all—so we might as well not even try.

I'll let you in on another secret, though: I don't think anybody can just sit down at their desk and have beautiful prose flow from their fingertips. First drafts are meant to be just that—the first in a sequence of drafts, which get progressively better. Becker (2007:55) calls the first draft a spew draft, meaning that it's the draft where you just spew out everything you can think of.[34] "Spew" is such an ugly word that the connotation is exactly right: a spew draft is an ugly thing that splatters all over the page.

If spew drafts are so ugly, should they be avoided? Absolutely not. Spew drafts are necessary, lovely creatures. Spew drafts serve a vital function: they get the thoughts from your head to the page. And once you've got something written down, you've got something you can shape, mold, and edit into a thing of beauty.

---

34. Lamott has a chapter titled "Shitty First Drafts," and I've also heard it called a "mad draft" or a "sacrificial draft."

So just do it. Work out a draft of your outline, choose a section to work on, and then just type out everything that's in your head that's relevant to the topic. Sometimes when I'm really having trouble I write in a super-colloquial style, almost like I'm talking to myself. I also sometimes type in comments to myself like "boy is that stupid" just so that I'll remember that I need to come back to something. Once I've got some kind of mess on the page, I can rework it. I can go back, clean up the prose, uncontract my contractions, delete the comments to myself, and generally work on making it into a coherent piece of prose. I can also spot the places where I was illogical, where I need to do more work, or where I need more support for my arguments. All of this is part of the self-editing process, but it can't be done until there's something to edit, and that's what the spew draft gives you.

I do, however, recommend not letting anybody see your spew drafts. They should be reserved for the privacy of your own home or office. Clean them up before inflicting them on anyone. Sometimes students give me their spew drafts, acknowledging that that's what they are, and I generally find that it's not worth my while to try to decipher the mess. It's best to only give second (or later) drafts to your readers.

Perfectionism

Perfectionism can keep you from starting or finishing projects. At the simplest level, it can manifest as a feeling that what you write isn't going to be perfect so you might as well not write anything at all (causing writer's block, discussed in the next section.) Conversely, it can cause you to get too attached to your own prose. Sometimes writers become irrationally defensive of a particular turn of phrase or sentence or even a type of organization, and all the well-intentioned advice in the world can't get them to change it. I find myself doing this sometimes, and the only way I can get myself to stop it is to make fun of myself. I say, "Okay, Monica, your writing is so *perfect* that you can't change one *precious* word of it," and things like that. Pretty soon I see that I'm being stubborn and that the relevant passage really does need to be changed. I think this clinging behavior sometimes comes from a deeply concealed laziness—after all, it's a lot easier to decide something is too perfect to change than to work on changing it.

Perfectionism can also cause the inability to let go of an entire manuscript. Some people have no trouble getting started, writing a spew draft, editing it, giving it to various readers for comments, doing more editing . . . and more . . . and more . . . , and then they're just never able to declare the piece finished. This isn't usually a terrible problem with term papers, since one generally has a fixed deadline and the paper just has to be turned in on a certain date. But it can be a dreadful problem with articles written for publication, and you need to watch out for it. I've seen this problem with untenured professors who needed to get those lines on their CVs (meaning that they needed to develop a longer list of publications so that they could get tenure), but who just couldn't let go of an article and move on to the next one. Of course every piece of writing will go through multiple drafts, and it goes without saying that you should strive to make everything you write the best it can be, but you also have to know when to say "Enough!" It's a bitter fact about the academic world that we are judged on the quantity of work that we produce—not just the quality—and you simply have to adjust to the pace that's expected of you. While quantity of work isn't as much of an issue for graduate students as it is for untenured faculty, expectations are constantly rising about how many publications a successful job applicant will have, making this important at the ABD level too.[35]

So you have to strike a balance: be a relentless reviser of your work, but learn how to recognize that a piece is finished. If you can't decide whether it is or not, show it to someone and ask them specifically whether they think it's ready to send out, and if not, what exactly it would need to have done to it to be ready. Watch for warning signs like excessive re-editing and the feeling that just one more check of the literature might yield the perfect reference that you need to really nail your argument. Make your work excellent but not excessive.

Writer's Block

The primary image I've always had of someone with writer's block is a sad and miserable creature who really wants to write, but for some mysterious reason is unable to do it. I picture someone tied to a chair with their computer only a few feet away, but they just . . . can't . . . reach . . . it.

All joking aside, some people do experience something difficult and real which we can describe by this expression. In many cases it's a cover term for a large set of avoidance behaviors that can come from all sorts of sources. They may be insecure about whether they can really write anything worthwhile, they may be a little bit bored with the topic, or they may not be good at prioritizing the many things they have to do. Clearly there is some psychological issue that stops them from getting the work of writing started and finished.

If you find yourself unable to write, sit down and examine the problem. Sometimes giving something a name gives us an excuse not to really think about what's going on—if we call it "writer's block," we imply that it's beyond our control. *It's not my fault I can't get this stupid paper written! I suffer from this terrible syndrome!* For most of us, recognizing our avoidance behaviors and realizing that they are controllable is enough to get us through the tough times when we really just don't want to do the writing we have to do.

---

35. ABD stands for "All But Dissertation," a term for someone who has completed all of the requirements for their degree except the final one. See chapter 8 for discussion.

I don't mean to minimize the truly debilitating state that some people can get into when it comes to writing, though. If the suggestions that I make just don't solve the writing problems you have, you should consult a professional. Don't let yourself sit around feeling like a failure—take the initiative to get some help. If you don't, you won't be able to finish your paper, or worse, your degree. It's as simple as that. (Of course, for some people, that may *be* the problem—they actually don't want to be in the program that they're in, or in any graduate program at all. This is another thing that a professional could help you to figure out.) The key is to take action, whether it's the relatively simple ideas that books on writing suggest, or talking to someone who is an expert on these problems and can provide some one-on-one counseling.

Draft Groups and Writing Buddies

At the risk of being repetitive, I want to say again that getting feedback from your peers is absolutely essential to a successful graduate (and post-graduate) career. Develop this habit early and keep doing it for as long as you remain in the academic world.

Specifically, you should try to develop a small group of friends who agree to read each other's work and provide constructive criticism. I say "friends" and "*constructive* criticism" because at this stage you don't need cutting, devastating criticism. That can come later, or from your professors, or if you're lucky not at all. This should be a supportive environment in which you're not afraid to expose your first attempts at writing like a linguist.

I've heard such groups called "draft groups" and "writing buddies." It doesn't matter what you call it—you can make up your own name whose significance is only clear to the members of the group if you want. You can organize it in any fashion that makes sense to you. One tip I would suggest, though, is to give the group some structure so that it doesn't disintegrate. You might agree on regular meetings, a maximum time to get someone's work read, a protocol for comments, or whatever you like. The key is to make sure that you keep it up, and don't let it fall by the wayside along with diets and exercise plans.

I can hear you whining already: *But I'm embarrassed!* Tough love time: GET USED TO IT. You're going to have to show your work to others eventually, and this really the easiest way to get used to that. Isn't it better to have your friends gently tell you what's wrong with your argument, rather than having your professor rip it apart, or worse, having an audience member at a conference publicly let you know where you went wrong?

I have a set of people that I send manuscripts to when I'm ready for a first round of comments. I still feel embarrassed when I send the manuscript out, and I feel a terrible fear in the pit of my stomach when I get the comments back. But even when the comments are negative, I'm grateful and I know that the person has my best interests at heart. This, in fact, leads us to the next section . . .

Interpreting Comments and Taking Criticism

It's hard enough to show your work to others. It's even harder to take their criticism. The crucial thing to do is to take a deep breath and try to evaluate the comments dispassionately. You can't be defensive and you can't be defeatist. If you just get mad, call the person some nasty name, and reject their comments out of hand, there's something wrong. On the other hand, if you get horribly depressed, put the manuscript away, and never look at it again, something else is wrong. Sometimes you need to wait a couple of days after you've first read the comments, and then read them again so that you can deal with them without overreacting. Look at it this way: even if the person's comments are completely off the wall and they totally misunderstood what you were getting at, you bear some responsibility. Your writing must not have been clear enough, and at the very least you need to do some revision so that another reader won't make the same mistakes in interpretation.

A common reaction to receiving comments is a sense of being overwhelmed. Many professors (and I know I'm guilty) cover their students' papers in comments, giving them a sense that they'll never be able to satisfy the prof. If you feel overwhelmed, apply the bird by bird method to dealing with the comments. If the person who read your work didn't do so, go through and number their individual points. Then go through them one by one, checking them off as you take care of them. This will help you to whittle down a seemingly impossible task to a more manageable one.

What if you honestly think a comment is wrong? I would recommend discussing it with the person who wrote the comment in that case. One approach I've advised my students to take is to go through my comments on their papers checking off the suggestions and corrections they've taken care of, and then to make a list of any they haven't taken care of, with an explanation of why they haven't done it. They then bring this list to me, and we discuss the issue. Usually it turns out that there was some misunderstanding on someone's part—either I didn't understand what they meant, or they didn't understand my comment. Of course sometimes you will just disagree, and in that case you have to figure out on a case-by-case basis how to handle it.

Whatever you do, don't ignore your professor's comments. I get absolutely livid when I get a second draft that contains problems I commented on in the first draft. It makes me feel like I wasted my time reading it the first time around.

What I've said above applies not only to peers' and professors' comments; it also applies to reviewers' reports for journals. When you get to the point of submitting articles to journals, you will go through the exact same thing, except that usually the comments come from anonymous reviewers. (See chapter 7 for more on this.) You should apply the same principles to reviewers' reports as you do to the comments you get from friends and professors. Take them seriously, do what you can about them, and move forward.

Exercise 10: Outline an Article

1. Go back to the three articles you used for exercise 8 and create several outlines for each one:

    a. Create an outline based on just the information in the abstract or introduction.

    b. Create an outline that shows just the section and subsection headings in the article, using the wording that the author used in the headings.

    c. Create an outline that shows the main ideas in the article. Include notes about where groups of data and examples are presented, and what sort of data or examples they are (e.g., statistical summaries of all results, example sentences from French and Portuguese, etc.).

2. How is each outline different? Which outline would you find it easiest to start from if you were writing the article, and why?

Exercise 11: Practicing Criticism

Do this exercise with a partner. Each of you must find a short article that you've read and did not find well-written or well-argued. Ask around for recommendations of bad or flawed articles if you can't think of anything.

1. Write a set of detailed comments on the article, trying to be as nasty and mean as you can (within the realm of reasonableness, of course—don't go off the deep end).

2. Trade articles and comments and redo your partner's comments, turning their comments into constructive criticism. Watch for misinterpretations, expressions like "fails to" or "doesn't know," and personal attacks.

3. Compare your original comments to your partner's revisions.

6 Conferences

In chapter 2, you read about conferences as a way to learn about and participate in the field. This chapter addresses the process of presenting your own research at a conference: submitting an abstract to a conference, creating a handout and giving a conference paper, presenting a poster, and helping to host a conference.

Finding an Appropriate Conference

Conferences are publicized through a "call for papers." These are essentially advertisements for conferences. If you're on the Linguist List, you'll see lots and lots of calls for papers.

A call for papers usually includes (at least) the following information: the dates and location of the conference; the topic, theme, or orientation of the conference; the names of any invited speakers; the length of time allotted for papers; what to include in your submission (e.g., the number of pages or words allowed, whether you can append an extra page with data); the address to send the abstract to; and a deadline.[36] Sometimes they'll also include information on preregistration for the conference, the date by which submitters will be notified of acceptance or rejection, and the address of the conference website.

When you have a paper that you're ready to present at a conference, you should look for a conference that fits your paper. It might be one that has a theme that fits your topic, one that is intended for papers within the theoretical framework that you use, one that advertises itself as a conference on a particular approach to linguistics in general or to a subfield of linguistics, or one that is specific to a language, a language family, or the languages of a geographic area. If you're not sure what conference to submit to, talk to your advisor, other professors, and your fellow graduate students. There's also a handy list of linguistics conferences at www.unc.edu/linguistics/confinfo.html, provided by the Linguistics Department at UNC-Chapel Hill.

Some conferences are less stress-inducing than others. There is an annual linguistics graduate student conference that might be a good place to start (its call for papers is usually posted on the Linguist List). My advice is to start small

---

36. Very occasionally there are no instructions about the length or type of abstract required. In that case, use your best judgment. I would generally keep it to a single page.

(maybe with a local conference, to minimize stress), but another professor in my department advises the opposite, arguing that it's a waste of time to present at minor conferences. As always, when you get conflicting advice, do what seems the most sensible to you (or what your advisor tells you to do).

The LSA annual meeting is the largest general linguistics conference in the United States, and many graduate students present there as a way of getting some visibility as they go on the job market. (The same applies to the major conferences for applied linguistics and languages: TESOL, AAAL, and MLA.) This is a very good idea, and something you should consider once you get used to presenting your work in public.

Writing and Submitting an Abstract

Writing Your Abstract

In an ideal world, we would all have fully written papers that we would base our abstracts on when submitting to a conference. But this is very rarely what happens in the real world. Instead, we usually write abstracts based on ideas and data, hopefully with a rough sketch of a paper either in our computers or at least in our heads. It's important not to write a promissory note—that is, an abstract that says, "I plan to look at X and find out whether Y is the case." An abstract like this will usually get rejected, since conference organizers don't want to get stuck with a paper that says, "I looked at X, but Y was not the case, so I have nothing to say" (or worse, with someone who withdraws at the last minute because their paper didn't work out). Before you write a conference abstract you need to have a good, solid hypothesis with data to back it up, even if you don't have the paper already written.

The structure of your abstract should essentially be the structure of your proposed paper. If space permits, you can even use numbered headings (like in a paper), but whether you use headings or not, it still should be organized like you plan to organize the paper. (Naturally this might change as you get to the actual writing stage, but try for good organization even at the beginning stages.)

Once you've organized the abstract, the goal is to reduce the argument you want to make to its essentials. You have to find a way to get your point across with a minimum of prose, but without losing the crucial elements of the argument.[37] Writing a good abstract is an art form, and it takes practice.

---

37. To see why clarity is so important, consider the following: Amy Dahlstrom, a former member of the LSA program committee (which makes the decisions on abstracts for the annual conference) told me that they often get 400–500 abstracts a year, and that the program committee has a short time to read and evaluate all of them. She said, "If your points aren't immediately clear and understandable to linguists who may be in other branches of the field, no one will have time to puzzle out your intended meaning."

The LSA has posted some very helpful information on writing abstracts at www.lsadc.org/info/abstract-models.cfm. A phonetician and a syntactician each took a real abstract from their area that they considered very well-written, and first explained what made them good abstracts. Then they rewrote them as bad abstracts (with permission, of course), and annotated them with an explanation of what made them bad. These are very instructive, and I highly recommend taking a look at them.

There are several other online guides to writing linguistics abstracts: www.unc.edu/linguistics/confinfo.html (scroll to the very bottom of the page, after the listing of conferences), web.clas.ufl.edu/users/wiltshir/abstract.htm, and www.linguistics.ucsb.edu/faculty/bucholtz/sociocultural/abstracttips.html.

Components of a Linguistics Abstract

The following list is not intended to be a plan for an abstract; that is, with the exception of the title, its order is not intended to mimic the order that the elements of an abstract should appear in. These are instead the bases that an abstract needs to cover. The ordering of elements is up to you.

Title

The title should be concise and to the point. One common mistake that beginners often make is that they don't think carefully about what to call their papers, and end up with a title that doesn't really describe what the paper does. The title should indicate, where relevant, the problem addressed, the language in question, an approach, and/or a theoretical perspective.

Statement of the Problem and Hypothesis

State the problem clearly, and then state your hypothesis about a solution to the problem clearly and concisely, right up front. Don't hide either of these halfway down the page. Typical ways to do this are: "This paper shows that . . ."; "In this paper, I show that . . ."; and "The analysis proposed here establishes that . . ."

Data

Obviously you can't give mountains of data in a short abstract. Give only what is absolutely necessary to make your point. Choose clean, clear examples, and make sure that they are well integrated into the abstract (review the section on introducing examples in chapter 4). Don't assume that the reviewers know the language or the data—explain what's going on. Finally, if you have the space to do it, indicate the source of the data.

Context

Make the scholarly context of your contribution clear. Why is this problem important? What theoretical framework are you using (and, where relevant, what variant of it)? What scholarly debate are you contributing to? Who has already addressed this problem? This can often be done very briefly, e.g., "Using Feature Geometry, as developed by Clements (1985) and others, we see that . . ." or "Since Paul (1886), historical linguists have debated whether . . ."

Methodology

This is only necessary when the methodology is relevant. A syntax abstract, for example, generally does not need a methods section. A quantitative study, however, does need this information. Check with your advisor if you're not sure about this.

Solution

You must provide a solution to the problem that you're addressing or generalizations about the data that you're describing. Lay this out explicitly—don't hint at it. Say how you account for the problem posed by the data, and explain why your account is preferable to others (assuming there are others). Don't submit an abstract unless you know at least in general terms what solution you will propose.

Submitting Your Abstract

Once you've written your abstract, be sure to have several people read it before you submit it. Abstracts, like papers, need to go through several drafts, and the best way to fine-tune your abstract is to get comments on it from your peers and from your advisor.

It's especially important that your advisor read your abstract before you submit it, since your presentation will, to some extent, reflect on his or her abilities as an advisor, and thus on his or her reputation in the field. If you send out something that's really bad or even just flawed in some obvious way, the readers are going to wonder what's wrong with your advisor. For this reason I require my students to show me all abstracts that they plan on submitting.

When you're ready to actually submit your abstract, be sure to read the instructions on the call for papers very carefully. Make sure that you have followed the length requirement scrupulously. Do you have to put the word count at the bottom of the abstract? (Some conferences require this.) Should you leave your name off the abstract itself? (Usually you should.) Follow all formatting requirements provided by the call for papers, and do not assume that your abstract deserves to be (or will be) treated as an exception to any of those requirements

And above all, be sure to send it in on time—many conferences will reject late abstracts out of hand.

There are three conventions about submitting abstracts you should pay attention to: First, it is frowned upon to submit an abstract based on something you have already published or had accepted for publication. The point of a conference in general is to present new ideas that have not yet been published.

Second, avoid submitting the same abstract to more than one conference at a time. If you do this, and your paper gets accepted at more than one, I recommend that you withdraw from all but one conference, and only give the paper at one. That is, in my opinion, you should not give the same paper more than once.[38] There are some exceptions to this. Sometimes an author might give a preliminary version of a paper at a small conference, and a more polished and expanded version at a larger conference. One can also give more than one paper on the same topic when the approach is different, or when the papers focus on different aspects of the same problem. And if you know for a fact that the audiences will be completely different at each conference, you might give somewhat similar papers at each one.

Third, most conferences allow only one abstract per individual (plus in some cases a coauthored paper). You might think that submitting twelve abstracts to the same conference would increase your chances of acceptance, but it's actually very annoying to conference organizers, and being annoying is not the way to get an acceptance.

Creating a Handout

Once your abstract is accepted (congratulations!), you will have to write your paper and construct a handout. The handout is what people will take with them when they leave your talk, and it's very important that it make a good impression. Many linguists use PowerPoint for their presentation, but paper handouts are still valuable for people to take notes on and carry off with them to remind them of your talk. Just make sure that your handout and your slides have the same material, so your audience does not have to split their attention in too many directions.[39]

Colleagues in other fields are often surprised to hear that linguists can't give a talk without a handout or slides. But of course it makes sense that we need them—it would be pretty hard to follow data from unfamiliar languages without having the examples in front of you. Laying such examples out clearly is a very important aspect of handout design.

---

38. Linguists have varying opinions on this, so check with your advisor.

39. Bruce Fraser and Geoffrey Pullum have written a very useful "Guidelines for Giving an LSA Paper" (www.lsadc.org/info/meet-papguide.cfm) which complements my advice on handouts and delivering talks.

However, handouts contain much more than examples. The sections below discuss what to include, handout design, and how many copies to make.

What to Include

Remember that it's much harder to comprehend an orally-delivered paper than it is to comprehend a paper that you read by running your eyes over it. (When you read, you can go back and reread if you lose the thread. There is no instant replay at a conference.) The handout is there, then, to help the audience follow what you're saying. It has to contain enough information to make the paper easy to follow, but not so much that the handout itself is a distraction.

It may seem obvious, but I'm going to say this anyway: the handout should be laid out in the same order as the talk. If you hop around on the handout ("Now turn back to page two"), you'll just confuse and irritate people.

When you do a trial run of your paper, ask your test audience to give you comments on your handout as well as on the talk itself. Ask them if the handout gave them enough information, or if there was anything else that should have been included. Ask too if there was anything that was unnecessary and should be deleted.

The minimum that should be included in a handout is your identifying information, the examples (and any abbreviations used), and any figures, graphs, or tables that you refer to.

Identifying Information

Figure 6.1 shows two ways that I've done a heading for conference handouts:

Negators and Negation in Menominee

Monica Macaulay
University of Wisconsin-Madison
mmacaula@wisc.edu

34th Algonquian Conference
Queen's University
October 25, 2002

MONICA MACAULAY   WORKSHOP IN GENERAL LINGUISTICS
mmacaula@wisc.edu   UNIVERSITY OF WISCONSIN-MADISON
                                   FEBRUARY 25, 2005

What Algonquian Can Tell Us about Prominence Hierarchies

Figure 6.1. Sample Handout Headings

It's important to put your email address on the handout (either in the heading or at the very end of the handout), so that people can get in touch with you if they are interested in discussing your ideas further. It's also important to put the date and the name of the conference on the handout, in case someone wants to refer to it at a later date and needs to remember when and where you gave the paper.

Examples

Include all of your examples, in the order that you discuss them. There is nothing more frustrating than searching a handout for an example that a speaker has read (or worse, referred to), and not finding it.

If you use any abbreviations in the glosses to your examples, put them on the handout too. I would suggest putting them on the first page—either in a footnote or a preliminary section—because otherwise people may not realize that they are there until the talk is over.

Figures and Graphs

These should be included on the handout if your paper includes them. Make sure that they are numbered and titled—don't just leave them floating with no explanation.

Rules and Constraints

If you formulate any rules or constraints in your paper, you should include them on the handout so that the audience can remember them.

Quotes and Definitions

If you're going to read a lengthy quote or give a definition that is important to the point of your paper, you might want to include that on the handout. These can be hard for the audience to follow and remember, and as a listener it's nice to be able to check back and refresh one's memory if necessary.

Section Headings

Including these helps the audience follow the organization of your paper. They aren't necessary, but can be a handy guide.

Main Points

Many people put the main points that they make in their paper on the handout. This is especially useful if, after the conference, an audience member wants to work through the presentation again. If the handout contains only examples, it can be hard to remember what the point of the paper was.

Be careful, though, not to put too much of your paper on your handout. It's very easy to go too far in this direction, which can have the unfortunate consequence that the audience sits and reads your handout instead of listening to you. Also avoid phrasing everything identically in the talk and in the visual materials, for the same reason. A good approach is to distill your main points into short bulleted items. Overall handout length varies a lot, but is typically five to ten pages.

If you know counterexamples to your argument, be honest and up-front about that. I once saw a paper where the authors included a section at the end of their handout titled "work in progress," which I figured out from their discussion was really about known counterexamples. That counts as work in progress (assuming they intended to continue working on those counterexamples), but it is better to acknowledge problems more openly.

References

It is important to include most or all of your references on the handout. These can be in a smaller font than the rest of the handout to make them fit.

Handout Design

The content of your paper is, of course, the most important thing about your talk. Nonetheless, the design of your handout does matter. A messy and disorganized handout will detract from your talk, and in the worst case, may cause people to get confused and respond more harshly than they otherwise would. Conversely, getting carried away with fancy graphics and neat little symbols can also detract from your presentation. Too many bells and whistles can be a distraction, and thus a liability. You want people to pay attention to you, not your handout, and clarity is crucial. As long as your handout is clear and to the point, you can consider it a success.

Handouts inherently waste paper (many get thrown away, even for the best talk), so most of us try to conserve a bit. Most people copy the handout back-to-back, and people often print the handout using the two-up or two-to-one feature on their printer. These can look quite sharp, especially with a border, but be sure that the type is still readable. If the type size gets reduced too much, your audience (especially the older members) may not be able to read it.

How Many Copies?

It's always hard to decide how many copies to make. On the one hand, you want to have enough for everyone, but on the other hand you don't want to waste reams of paper by making too many. One way to solve this is to ask the organizers of the conference what kind of attendance they are expecting, and thus how many handouts they would advise making. If there are, say, two concurrent sessions, estimate that about half of the total will attend your talk. In the long run, it's far better to have too many than too few, since people are often extremely frustrated (and may even walk out) if they can't get a handout.

Furthermore, sometimes people who didn't attend will pick up a handout after the fact, or people who do attend will grab an extra to take to a colleague. Look at it as a relatively inexpensive investment in your career.

PowerPoint

Most of my advice about handouts applies to PowerPoint presentations too. You'll need to include essentially the same information: the title, your name and affiliation, your email address, examples, etc. The key difference is that you need to keep each slide focused on a single, main point. Make sure the font size is large enough that people can read it from a distance, and don't clutter the slides with a lot of detail. If your presentation really rests on presenting results in tables or charts, make them as simple and clean as possible.

While you're giving the presentation, refer to the material on the slides but don't just read it verbatim. The audience can read silently faster than you can read out loud, so they'll get ahead of you and then have to wait impatiently for you to finish. Instead, use the material on the slides as prompts, and explain what each slide shows. A nice trick is to number the slides, which helps to identify a particular slide that might come up in the question period.

Delivering a Paper

Linguists are rarely trained in delivering papers, although this is an important aspect of our academic lives. This section gives you some tips on the performance of a paper.

This comes up again below, but I want to make sure you note it from the outset: it is critically important that you rehearse giving your paper.[40] First deliver it to your mirror or your cat. Then when you feel more confident, deliver it to some friends. Many departments schedule dry runs for all students who are giving a paper at a conference, and I think this is a good idea. Not only will it help you to make sure your paper is the correct length, it will give you a chance to get feedback from a sympathetic audience before taking the paper out into the uncharted territory of a conference. The audience can give you comments on the content, as well as on your delivery. Both kinds of comment can make the actual delivery more successful.

---

40. I like John Goldsmith's line on this issue: "It is an egregious faux pas not to prepare an oral presentation and not to spend all the time that it requires" (Goldsmith et al. 2001:70).

When practicing your paper, pay attention to intonation. It can be helpful to mark words or phrases that you want to stress, and sometimes even to mark the intonation you want on a particular sentence.

Read or Talk or Something in Between?

Many people in linguistics—at least to some extent—*read* their orally-delivered papers. That is, they have a prepared text, and they read from it. Now, common wisdom has it that this is a bad practice—in fact, outsiders are often shocked to learn how common this is in our field. The preferred method is supposedly to "talk" one's paper, informally. Let's first consider some pros and cons of reading a prepared text:

In Favor of Reading Your Paper

- It will keep you on track—that is, you will not go off on tangents.

- Your arguments will be organized and will follow in a logical order (assuming you write the paper that way).

- You won't forget what you wanted to say, or what the details were. This can happen to people sometimes when they are really nervous, but it won't happen if you have a prepared text in front of you.

- You can time a written text. If you're just going to "talk" your paper, it's very hard to keep to the specified time limit. I've seen a lot of people go over their time or not be able to finish what they wanted to say because it took them much longer to explain something than they thought it would.

Against Reading Your Paper

- It's harder for the audience to follow you (especially if you read too fast).

- The audience can get bored, which means they won't pay attention.

Luckily, there are various ways of finding a middle ground. One way is to "talk" the paper from the handout or slides. This requires that the handout or slides be fairly thorough, and more than just a collection of examples. You can always annotate your copy to make sure you remember all the necessary details. Another approach is to have a very detailed list of points instead of actual prose, ordered in the way that your points are ordered in the full paper, and then talk from that. A third way is to have a fully written-out text, but to just rely on it for direction. After practicing your talk repeatedly, you can get to know it so well that when it comes time to present the paper you can glance at a paragraph and then present its content in a more spontaneous fashion. All of these methods take some confidence, but not as much as completely winging it does. Whatever you do, don't forget about keeping to your allotted time.

It's your decision whether to "talk" (to whatever degree) or read your paper. If you do decide to read it, there are several ways you can make it easier on the audience.

Suggestions for Reading

- Write the oral version of the paper in a casual style, with contractions and colloquial terms (where appropriate). This way it sounds more like you're talking than reading.

- Look up frequently to make eye contact with the audience (but be careful not to lose your place).

- Use normal conversational intonation—don't read in a monotone.

- Read at a normal speed. It's very common for people to speed up when they're nervous—make sure you don't go too fast.

Examples: To Read or Not To Read

When people know that their paper might run over the time limit, sometimes they just skip the examples. I think this is a very bad idea—the audience needs a moment to digest the examples (especially if they are in an unfamiliar language). If you're reading along and just say, "As examples (55) and (56) show, my theory is brilliant, blah-blah-blah," your audience may stop listening to you while they read the examples. Then they have to tune back in and try to figure out what they missed.

If you do read the examples (which I recommend), read them fairly quickly, and don't read the glosses unless there's something in particular that you want to point out. If you feel you have to skip the examples, at least pause for a moment to give the audience a chance to work through them.

The Time Limit

Nothing makes a session chair (not to mention subsequent speakers and the audience) more upset than a presenter who goes over his or her time limit. Practice delivering your paper—time it (repeatedly) and make sure it's the right length. Most session chairs will let you run over a minute or two into your question period, but will then cut short the questions to stay on schedule.[41]

---

41. One of my favorite examples of not paying attention to the time limit was a young student who, upon being advised that his time was almost up, said, "Five minutes left? Whoo-hoo, in that case I have to cruise."

"I'm Done Now"

Sometimes speakers finish their paper and then just look up at the audience. Nobody knows what to do: "Are they done?" "Should we clap?" There's often a long, awkward silence at this point, with everyone looking and feeling uncomfortable. The situation is only made worse if the speaker mutters something like: "Well, I guess that's about all I have to say" (or as I have actually heard: "I'm sorry to have taken up so much of your time," "I'll try to come up with a better analysis next time," and "I guess I should kind of stop now before I depress everybody"). So instead, when you're done, just say "Thank you." That way the audience knows that they can clap, the session chair can open the floor for questions (or go on to the next speaker), and everybody feels happy.

The Question Period

Many first-time paper presenters (and some of us old-timers too) get more nervous about the question period than about actually delivering the paper. Here are some points to remember: (a) You've been thinking about this topic for quite a while, so you probably *will* know the answer to whatever you're asked. But, (b) you don't have to know *everything*. If someone asks you something you don't immediately know the answer to, think about it carefully (it's okay if some seconds pass while you think). There may very well be something that bears on the question that you *can* say, even if you don't answer it precisely. Note that I'm NOT recommending that you say something irrelevant because you don't know the answer and want to fill up the time! That's usually very transparent, and never a successful strategy.

But what if you absolutely don't know what to say? In that case, you can say something like: "That's a very interesting question, and I'll have to give it some thought," or "Actually, I don't know the answer to that. Thank you—I'll look into it," or (if someone asks if you have read some particular article and you haven't) "Thank you for the reference." Keep in mind that it's much better to admit your ignorance than to try to pretend you know something you don't know—people can usually tell what's up in the latter case.

It's a good idea to have a pen and some paper with you so that you can take notes on people's questions and comments. Sometimes it's hard to remember the questions after you've given a paper—you might be in a bit of a daze afterwards. If you don't feel like you can take notes while also answering questions, assign the job to a friend who's going to be in the audience. You don't want to forget what people say about your paper because you may want to incorporate it when you write the paper up for publication. And be sure to thank members of the audience at the conference (by group or by name) in your first footnote.

While the public question period only lasts a few minutes, people may approach you later at the conference to ask questions or continue a discussion about your paper. This is a great opportunity to make contacts and share ideas. Make some simple business cards to bring to conferences to make it easier to exchange contact details.

A Note on Etiquette

Conferences are divided into sessions, which usually consist of three or four papers (although the number may vary). You should attend the entire session in which your paper is to be given; arriving just before your paper and leaving just after it is very rude to the other speakers. It implies that you don't find their contributions interesting enough to stay for. This applies whether all of the speakers are seated at a table in the front of the room, facing the audience, or whether they are seated at random among the audience.

Poster Sessions

The conference poster session is well-established in other fields, but is a relatively recent innovation in most areas of linguistics. In a poster session, presenters gather in a room supplied with large easels or other means of displaying posters for some scheduled period of time (two or three hours is typical). The audience walks through the room, engaging in conversation with the author of any poster which catches their eye.

This is obviously a very different means of presenting research results than the more usual orally-delivered paper, and works especially well for certain types of topics, particularly those that lend themselves to clear visual representation and summary. A project with a small number of graphs or tables which concisely illustrate the point of the research is ideal for a poster presentation.

Poster sessions have a number of advantages. First and foremost is the fact that the presenter can interact directly with individual audience members, conversing about the topic instead of lecturing. This not only allows for potentially clearer explanation of the topic (tailored to each individual listener), but also allows for immediate feedback and interaction. This kind of interaction can also lead to opportunities for networking that might not have arisen in a conventional session. Finally, the audience can come see the posters at any point during the session, allowing for greater flexibility in their schedules. In fact, many conferences leave the posters up for longer than just the scheduled session so that even if a viewer misses the session they can still see the poster and seek out the author if they're interested enough in the topic.

The simple way to create a poster is to put up normal size sheets of paper which together fill the space of the poster. The alternative is to create an actual poster—that is, a single, large page containing all of the information. Various programs (e.g., PowerPoint, InDesign, Adobe Illustrator) allow you to design the poster as a single sheet. Be forewarned that it can be expensive to get the finished product printed if you take this route—the Digital Media Center at my university currently charges $5/square foot. (A typical poster is 3' × 4', which comes out to $60 at that rate.) This kind of poster, although expensive, looks vastly more professional than the simple method described at the beginning of this paragraph.

Either way, make sure that all of your text is in a very large font, easily readable from a few feet away. If you use a small font, and include too much detail, people will simply walk away instead of trying to put their noses right up to the poster to be able to read it. The headers should be in an even larger size type, so that they stand out from across the room. Colors should contrast and stand out, too. See www.lsadc.org/info/meet-poster.cfm for a very thorough guide to designing a poster, written by Kristen Syrett.

Ask the conference organizers if they will be providing thumbtacks or other means of hanging the posters, and bring your own if not. (You might want to bring your own in any case. One of my students says to bring lots; if you do, you will find yourself very popular among the other poster presenters.) Thumbtacks or pushpins are preferable to tape, since tape sometimes comes unstuck, and doesn't look very nice, either. The LSA also suggests binder clips, which don't put holes in your poster.

During the actual poster session, be prepared to discuss every aspect of your work. You should prepare a five- to ten-minute spiel about your topic for those who are interested in hearing more than just what is on the poster. It's also a good idea to take notes on the feedback that you get, since you may not remember everything that is discussed. Finally, many people create a handout to go along with the poster, so that viewers have something to take away with them. The handout can either contain exactly the information that's on the poster, or it can contain additional information that fills out what's on the poster itself. If people take a handout, that means that they will be able to discuss the poster further with you later. To facilitate this, you should include your contact info on the poster as well as on the handout.

Poster sessions are not for everybody, and do not fit every topic. But when done well they can provide an interesting alternative to the usual mode of presentation, and they are definitely gaining in popularity in our field.

Funding Your Trip

There aren't a lot of sources of funding for going to conferences, but there are a few. Some departments have funding they can offer to students who are giving a paper at a conference—it may be a fixed amount and may not cover all of your expenses, but it can help. Some of the bigger conferences offer a limited amount of financial help to graduate students. The LSA, for example, has offered a few travel awards in recent years, and they're always looking for volunteers to help with staffing, possibly in exchange for waiving the registration fee.

Hosting a Conference

Conferences are wonderful learning experiences, whether you deliver a paper or not. Putting on a conference is even more educational, but it is a huge amount of work, not to be undertaken lightly.

Should your department be hosting a conference, volunteer to help out. If possible, volunteer to read abstracts. I learned almost everything I know about what makes a good (or bad) abstract by reading abstracts for an annual meeting held in the department I did my graduate work in.

During the conference, you will have a natural reason to meet everyone present if you are one of the organizers or helpers. And don't just focus on the famous people—meeting other graduate students at a conference can provide you with lifetime friendships and useful future contacts.

Finally, if the proceedings are going to be published, volunteer to participate in some way. The process varies from conference to conference—sometimes the papers are extensively edited, and sometimes they are not. It's important to find out ahead of time exactly what is expected of volunteer editors by talking with the primary organizers, the publisher, and the editors from previous years. Working on a proceedings can be a great way to observe more experienced linguists go through the process of writing and revising, to interact with linguists you might otherwise not have met, and to make potentially useful contacts. (It can also be very time-consuming and frustrating if you have to deal with a recalcitrant author, although that's a learning experience in and of itself.) This kind of undertaking is a very good way to demystify the publication process for yourself, and you also get to put the experience on your CV.

Exercise 12: Handout Design

Choose a paper that you've read carefully.

1. Pretending that it's your own paper, devise a handout for it as if you were going to give it at a conference. Be sure to check over all of the points made above while constructing the handout.

2. Have your professor or someone knowledgeable about linguistics conferences take a look at your handout and give you some feedback.

7 Funding and Publishing Your Research

Anne Lamott on the Joys of Publishing

Seeing yourself in print is such an amazing concept: you can get so much attention without having to actually show up somewhere. While others who have something to say or who want to be effectual, like musicians or baseball players or politicians, have to get out there in front of people, writers, who tend to be shy, get to stay home and still be public. There are many obvious advantages to this. You don't have to dress up, for instance, and you can't hear them boo you right away. (Lamott 1994:xiv)

All academics know the expression "publish or perish," publications being the currency of the academic world. If you decide to take an academic job, you will be judged on the quality and (perhaps unfortunately) on the quantity of your publications throughout your career. They will play a significant role at those transition times: finding a job, getting tenure, getting promoted. You almost never get any money for publication, although some journals will give you a small reward like offprints (copies of your article in its published form) or even a free subscription for a year.[42] This chapter addresses the steps to getting published in the field of linguistics, from funding your research to its appearance in a journal—the key to not perishing.

Grant Proposals

Many graduate students are unaware of the fact that they are eligible to apply for a wide range of grants. Since money is so tight in colleges and universities these days, it's important to get in the habit of searching out relevant grants and to develop good grant-writing skills.

Although most linguists apply for and get some number of grants, linguistics is not like the hard sciences, where people's careers are truly dependent on the grants that they receive. Nonetheless, there is money to be had out there, and it can make doing your research significantly easier. Even a small grant can help

---

42. Journals in some other fields have a page charge for publication—that is, the author is charged a per-page amount to get their article published. To my knowledge, linguistics journals haven't adopted this practice . . . yet.

you buy equipment or travel to a fieldwork site or a library where you can do your research, so even the minor grants are worth applying for.[43]

There are many excellent guides to grant writing on the market, and this short section is intended to add some linguistics-specific information as a supplement to such guides. You should explore the written and electronic resources on grant writing for more information. A few useful electronic guides to start with are:

National Science Foundation (U.S.): Grant Proposal Guide
www.nsf.gov/publications/pub_summ.jsp?ods_key=gpg11001

National Endowment for the Humanities (U.S.):
Advice on Preparing Your Grant
www.neh.gov/grants/advice.html

Social Science Research Council (Canada): The Art of Writing Proposals
www.ssrc.org/publications/view/7A9CB4F4-815F-DE11-BD80-001CC477EC70

There are also a number of written guides to grant writing. An excellent one that was written by a linguist is Chapin (2004). Paul Chapin was a program officer for the NSF (National Science Foundation) for 25 years, so he knows the topic inside and out. In addition, most universities have a division or an office to help with grant writing; it is very important to get their advice and feedback as you prepare a proposal (at least for the really large ones).

The first step in grant writing is, of course, learning about the grants available to linguists. The Linguist List website has a "funding sources" page which lists a number of relevant grants, and grant availability is regularly announced on their mailing list. The LSA's website also has a grants page which provides a calendar of deadlines and a list of addresses of granting agencies.[44] For sources of government funding, Chapin (2004:39) recommends the Catalog of Federal Domestic Assistance (CFDA; www.cfda.gov). Huge catalogs of grants are also usually available in the reference rooms of most libraries (and online at many universities); consult the reference librarian to make the task of wading through them a bit easier. Finally, ask other linguists where they have gotten funding from, and for what.

Once you've zeroed in on a grant that you want to apply for, read through the eligibility criteria very carefully. Make sure that your project is really eligible: don't waste the granting agency's time—or your own—by applying for

---

43. Although grants do not "count" as much as publications do, they are usually considered a plus on the CV (see chapter 9), so in fact they are helpful to your career in more than just the financial sense.

44. This page is restricted to members only (you have to log in to access it)—another reason why you should join the LSA!

something with an inappropriate proposal. If you aren't sure, contact the granting agency and ask.[45]

In fact, it's a good idea to get in touch with the granting agency in any case. The grants officers are there for you to work with, and they often lament the fact that many applicants don't take advantage of their expertise and advice. Don't be shy: Just call or email the person, and start up a conversation by describing your proposed project and asking if they think it is worth submitting an application. Some grants officers will even read a draft before submission, which can give you a real edge over the competition.

When writing up your proposal, keep in mind all of the writing tips I've already covered. Make sure you organize, make sure you're clear, and make sure you consider your audience. There are at least three things that you will need to do in a grant proposal that you don't normally need to do in a paper. First, you have to establish that there is a need for the project to be done—that it is innovative and exciting. This will involve showing that it hasn't been done before, and explaining why it should be done. Make sure that part of explaining the need for the project is putting it in the broader context of the field. There are usually smaller and larger reasons for doing a particular research project, and you should talk about both types. In order to establish need, you have to do your homework; this is where having done the background research and having prepared a thorough bibliography is essential.[46]

Second, you must convince your audience that you are qualified to do this project. You can explain your background, showing that you have taken classes in the relevant area, have already done some preliminary research, etc. If language skills are required (say, if your proposal includes going to another country to do research), show that you already speak the language. (Don't say you plan on learning it—the promissory note approach will hurt you.) Some agencies require that you submit a CV (see chapter 9), so some of this information may be included on your CV and won't have to be elaborated. If the proposal requires letters of recommendation, your qualifications to do the research are something that your recommenders can also address. And if your project is experimental, it helps to have done a pilot study and to report the results of that.

Third, find out who your audience is. (This is a good question to ask the grants officer or other representative of the granting agency.) Some grant proposals are reviewed by committees made up of people from a number of

---

45. The large granting agencies have officers who specialize in particular areas. So, for example, the NSF has one person in charge of linguistics proposals, another in charge of the Documenting Endangered Languages program (DEL), etc. Smaller agencies may just have one person in charge of all of their programs. Contact information is usually included in the general information about the grant.

46. In fact, Chapin (2004:13–23) argues at some length that organizing and planning the project is a necessary step before even attempting to write a proposal.

different fields, and in such a case you have to write the proposal for that kind of audience. If the audience will include non-linguists, you will have to avoid jargon and explain your terminology in a way that you wouldn't have to for an audience of linguists.

More specifically, a grant proposal will have several components, usually laid out explicitly in the instructions, e.g., a project description, a biographical sketch (or CV), a budget, a budget justification, and so on. Chapin provides a useful list of what needs to go into the project description:

Elements of the Project Description (Chapin 2004:63–64)

- Conceptual foundations (the hypothesis)
- Survey of the literature
- Results of prior research (if applicable)
- Project design
- Significance (the intellectual and scientific contribution of the project)
- Broader impacts (the relevance of the project for education and society)
- Plan for dissemination of results

These project description elements closely follow the required elements in an NSF proposal. Other granting agencies may have other required elements, but this list provides a good starting point for organizing your proposal.

Despite some areas of overlap, the ability to write good grant proposals is distinct from the ability to write good research papers. Baron lists the following major mistakes to avoid in writing grant proposals:

Seven Deadly Sins of Proposal Writing (Baron 1987:165–167)

- The absence of theory
- The absence of clear-cut links between theory and research
- Methodological flaws or ambiguity
- The absence of close links to past, related work
- An absence of overall significance for the field
- Inappropriate or ambiguous plans for data analysis
- Proposing too much or proposing too little

After you've written a proposal, it would be a good idea to look it over carefully with each one of these "sins" in mind. If you think you've fallen into any of these traps, make sure you revise the offending part before you send it off.

A word (or two) on letters of recommendation: first, as always, make sure you give the person who will write the letter plenty of time. Don't wait until the last minute. Second, provide them with a copy of your proposal so that they know what you are planning on doing, and can write an informed and helpful letter. (This means that you can't wait until the last minute to write the proposal, either.) The recommender may also be able to give you suggestions about how to improve the proposal.

Making up the budget is often daunting. It's hard to know how to estimate expenses. Consult with someone local (e.g., the grants office at your university) and with the granting agency's representative to get some help on this. There are standard estimated rates for mileage and meals that you can use; this is much easier than trying to figure out what the actual costs might be. You might also have to make a few phone calls—for example, what does a hotel room cost where you're going?

If you're applying for a large grant, you will encounter the dreaded issue of overhead. Overhead is a chunk of money that universities take out of grants to cover administrative costs associated with the grant. It can run quite high— 50% of the total amount that you're asking for is not uncommon. But overhead is written into the grant; that is, you don't get the money you ask for and then lose half of it. Rather, you write that amount into the grant, and the big agencies know that it's part of what they have to give you. So if you're applying for $100,000, you just write in the $50,000 that the University would take, for a total of $150,000. Work closely with the grants office at your university to get this part figured out.

One last thing to know about applying for grants, especially big ones, is that most people get turned down on their first try. If you get turned down, try again on the next round. Find out what the objections to your project were, if they are willing to tell you, and fix the proposal accordingly. (If the agency is willing to send you reviews, request them.) Since most of us do at least some of the project even without funding, you can add in the progress that you've made to your second attempt, showing that it really is a viable undertaking.

Working Papers and Conference Proceedings

Working papers and conference proceedings are relatively easy ways to get published, but each has a very different status in the field. Working papers are informal publications (often compiled by student groups or departments) containing articles which present work in progress. They do not count for much as publications (because acceptance is generally fairly automatic), but can help you to get feedback on your work. Consider submitting your work to working papers series at other universities too—some are open to outside submissions.

Conference papers are, as you might guess, the published papers from a conference. I always advise my students that any paper that's good enough to be delivered at a conference is good enough (albeit in revised form) to be published. Some conferences make this easy for you by publishing a conference proceedings. In other words, getting the abstract accepted may guarantee you a publication. The importance of such a publication varies from conference to conference. One crucial question is whether the papers are refereed—that is, whether they are sent out to reviewers before being accepted for publication in the proceedings. Some proceedings just publish every paper given at the conference; others pick and choose. Obviously being refereed increases the prestige of the publication, since that means the paper has been judged worthy by (one hopes) a set of knowledgeable linguists.

Most of what I will have to say below about publishing in journals applies to working papers and conference proceedings as well. In general, follow the style sheet carefully, pay attention to the deadlines, and be sure to have others read your paper before sending it off. Keep in mind that a published paper is very different from a paper that you read aloud to an audience: you will have to do a great deal of revising to get the paper into publishable form. Don't expect to just be able to pop the paper you delivered into the mail to the editors of the volume. Revise it and go through another round of evaluation from your set of sympathetic readers before sending it to the editors.

Publishing an Article in a Journal

While conference proceedings are a great source of publications, journal articles are much more highly valued, especially when you are trying to get a job or tenure.[47] You will hear journals described as "refereed" or "peer-reviewed." Like the refereed conference proceedings discussed above, a refereed journal is one where the editor sends your manuscript out to two or three experts in the field (called referees, reviewers, or peer reviewers) to get their opinions on whether it should be published or not.

I participated in a graduate student panel on getting published at the 2010 LSA, and with the help of my fellow panelists, drew up the Getting Published flowchart in figure 7.1. In the sections which follow I discuss each of the stages in this flowchart.[48]

---

47. There has been a huge escalation of the expectations for people on the job market in the last decade or two. When I finished my dissertation in 1987, some job candidates had refereed journal articles on their CVs, but it certainly wasn't the norm. Now, however, most recent PhDs do have them (and often more than one). The expectations have risen, and you need to keep in mind that this is what you will be competing with.

48. Neal Whitman has posted a summary of the panel's discussion on his blog at literalminded.wordpress.com/2010/01/13/how-to-publish-a-scholarly-paper.

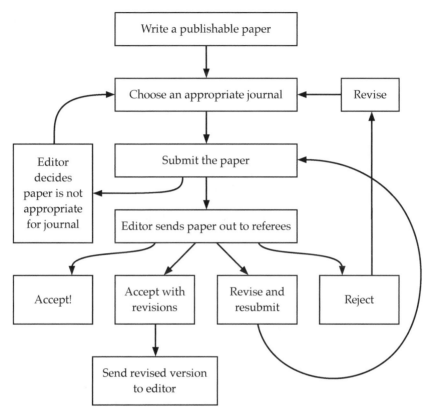

Figure 7.1. Getting Published

Writing a Publishable Paper

Since the focus of the flowchart is on getting a paper published, it almost assumes the first step—writing something publishable. But this is not a trivial matter, as I'm sure you can appreciate.

When I say "publishable," I really mean that. You don't want to enter the process until you have a highly polished, professional piece of scholarship to submit. Some people regard the initial submission as a chance to get serious feedback on a paper. You may get good feedback, but sending a paper out prematurely wastes the valuable time (and goodwill) of the reviewers and editor. So spend the extra time doing revisions before sending it out.

You may now be thinking, "But how will I know if my work is publishable?" Here is where you really need your group of advisors—your professors, your peers, and anyone else who can help you evaluate the contribution your paper makes. Sometimes you may be lucky and have a professor tell you that you should think about submitting something you've written, but you can't always wait for someone else to bring it up. If you think you have something publishable, go talk to your advisor, other professors, and your writing buddies, and see what they think about the idea.

Choosing a Journal

Just as it's important to choose an appropriate conference, it's important to choose an appropriate journal to submit your article to.[49] Be sure to consult with your advisor on this. People who have been in the field longer have a better idea of the theoretical stance and relative status of the journals in the field, and your advisor can help you figure out which journal is best for your paper (as well as which journal is most likely to accept it).

Once you've found a couple of likely possibilities, be sure to look over several issues of the journals in question. Many have a statement of their focus and goals in each issue or on their website. Also look at the composition of the editorial board for clues as to the orientation of the journal. Make sure that the journal is appropriate for your paper—if it isn't, the editor will just send it back without even sending it out for reviews, and this is a waste of everyone's time.

It is very important to remember that you can only submit to one journal at a time. Journal editors get very angry if they learn of double (or multiple) submission, and linguistics is a small enough field that multiple submissions do get caught.[50] The way it works is that you submit the paper to one journal, and if it gets rejected, then and only then do you go on to another. It's true that this is a lengthy process, but that's just how it is. Editors don't want to put in the time and work of sending a paper out for review only to find out that you've had the paper accepted somewhere else. Multiple submission is considered a grave academic sin, so don't do it under any circumstances.

Preparing Your Manuscript

Each journal has a style sheet, which usually tells you in excruciating detail how to format your article for submission. The style sheet is generally available on the journal's website.

---

49. The Linguist List has a listing of linguistics journals at www.linguistlist.org/pubs/tocs, which may be helpful to you if your library does not have a large selection.

50. This goes for submitting articles out of a published dissertation, too. The key point to remember is that any submission has to be original, and not previously published (although most journals make an exception for a working papers publication). The Notes to Contributors on the *Language* website (www.lsadc.org/info/pubs-lang-notes.cfm) has a typical statement of such a policy.

Information Provided in a Journal Style Sheet

- The name and email address of the person you should send your submission to. This is usually the main editor for articles, the review editor for reviews, etc. A few journals have separate editors for European submissions, or for other types of manuscript.

- What format you should submit your article in. Some journals have a submission website where you upload your article, instead of sending it by email.

- The required font size and line spacing (almost always 12-point and double-spaced).

- A page limit if there is one.

- Whether or not to include your name on the paper. Some journals tell the referees who wrote the paper, which is known as "blind" or "single-blind" reviewing, meaning that the referees know who you are but you don't know who they are. Other journals don't give the referees this information, in which case the process is known as "double-blind" reviewing—you don't know the referee's name and the referee doesn't know yours. Unless the referee specifically tells the editor that their identity can be revealed, you are never told who refereed your article.

- Other stylistic information, such as the treatment of emphasized words, the format for the references, etc.[51] Follow these instructions carefully, or—assuming your article is accepted—they will send it back and ask you to reformat it. It's a lot easier to just do it right the first time.

- Whether an abstract is required. This is different from a conference abstract, in that it's always written after the paper is finished, and often uses passages from the article verbatim (yes, you can plagiarize yourself in this context). If the journal you're submitting to requires an abstract, look at some already-published articles in the same journal to get a feel for what it should look like and how long it should be.

Prepare your paper carefully, following all of the guidelines given by the journal. It's important to fill in all the blanks and fix all the glitches you might have left in at an earlier stage. Make sure, for example, that all of your references

---

51. I've always thought it was a little silly to do all that formatting at the submission stage, since the precise style guidelines are really for the convenience of the publisher. While many journals do require submitted papers to be in the journal's official style, some only require that an article follow their style sheet when a final version is being prepared for publication, so check the journal's requirements carefully.

are complete (no missing page numbers or publishers), that the sources you refer to are all listed in the references section, that your example numbers are sequential, etc. You want this version to be completely professional.

Once you've got the paper ready to go, you will probably need to write a cover letter or email, unless you're submitting through an automated website. Address it to the editor, and say something very simple like: "Please consider the enclosed article, [title], for publication in [journal name]," or "I am submitting the enclosed article, [title], for consideration in [journal name]." Unless you have a specific reason to say something else, the cover letter does not have to say anything more.

What Happens after You Submit Your Manuscript

When the editor receives your paper, they will decide whether it is suitable for inclusion in the journal. If they decide that it is, they'll ask two or three people to act as referees. These people are chosen based on their experience, their knowledge of the theory you're working in, their knowledge of the data you discuss, and/or on their reliability. Some consider it acceptable to suggest a few names for readers, or to request that a particular person *not* serve as a reader, but I would avoid this in most cases because it really is the editor's call.

The referees who have agreed to read your paper do so, and write up a report for the editor. These differ in length but can range from one or two pages to many more, depending on how many comments they have for you.

Some editors will send you a note acknowledging receipt of your paper, and letting you know how long it ought to take to get a decision. If not, wait a few months, and then send a very polite email message asking the editor if they could let you know what the status of your paper is.[52] Don't be shy—it's the editor's responsibility to let you know what's going on, and if they don't, you have every right to ask. Of course, don't get too pushy, and don't bug them every week, but if a long period of time has gone by with no response, you have every right to inquire.

The Decision

Once the referees' reports are completed, the editor reviews them and makes a decision based on the advice of the referees and his or her own expertise. Some journals have an intermediate level of associate editors who read the reports and make a recommendation to the editor. There are usually four possible outcomes:

---

52. Some people have told me this is too long to wait; others have said it is not enough time. You should probably just ask your advisor what they think and follow their advice.

- **Accept.** You've hit the jackpot!
- **Accept with revisions.** This is the most common form of acceptance.
- **Revise and resubmit.** This is not an acceptance, but it is not a rejection either. The editor is telling you that your paper has real possibilities, but that it needs serious work. If you submit a revised version, it will be sent out for review again.
- **Reject.** Oh well.

It's pretty unusual to get a paper accepted with no suggested revisions (I'm not sure it's ever actually happened!). So if they ask you to make revisions, you should make them. Your paper has been accepted, but you need to remember that it has been accepted under the condition that you make certain changes. This is where it's essential to know how to accept criticism of your work (see the discussion in chapter 5). Most editors send the referees' reports to you no matter what the decision; you should try to think of them as constructive criticism even if they're harsh.

When I get an article accepted with suggested revisions, I work through the referees' reports, and revise my manuscript as much as I feel is necessary. Then I write a cover memo to go with it, detailing what I did and what I didn't do. I'm very specific: I say, "I took referee A's points 1, 2, and 3, but I did not follow their advice in 4." Then I explain *why* I did not do what they said in 4. If I have a good reason, the editor will usually accept it (although some editors are more willing to negotiate these points than others). It's not enough to say, "The idiot totally misinterpreted me, so I'm not making any changes." Even if it is true that the idiot misinterpreted you, you do need to make some changes so that it doesn't happen again with the next reader.

Now, what if you get the fourth option: total, utter rejection? First you may need to spend some time crying or ranting and raving.[53] When you've gotten that out of your system, work through the referees' reports. (If the editor didn't send them to you, contact the editor and request them.) Make substantial revisions to your paper, taking the referees' comments into account, and then submit it to another journal. I mean it. If your professor (or someone else) has encouraged you to publish the paper, then it's probably good enough to get published somewhere. Maybe it won't be in the top journal in your area, but as a graduate student, it's fine to publish in other journals. (It's fine as a professor, too, at least on occasion.) Just don't give up—it's worth it to keep trying, and it's a waste of all the energy you put into the paper to just throw it in the trash at this point.

---

53. Please do this in private. Don't force the editor, your advisor, or even your Facebook friends to witness it.

The Final Step

Assuming your paper is accepted with revisions, you return a revised version to the editor, and receive a contract in return. The contract will explain the journal's policy on copyright (they usually hold the copyright) and other matters. Sign it and send it back immediately, or you may delay publication of your article.

Finally, you will one day receive proofs in the mail. The proofs are copies of exactly what the article will look like when it is published, and you can only make small and essential changes at this point. You can't, for example, make any changes in content, or add sentences or paragraphs. Instead, you need to go over the proofs very carefully, looking for typos and errors, marking them as directed in the instructions.

If at all possible, get someone to help you check the proofs. The ideal situation is to have one person read out loud while the other follows along on the original. But if this isn't possible, get your original out and do a word-by-word comparison by yourself. It's tedious, but it will prevent embarrassing mistakes from appearing in print.

Luey (2010) provides a nice discussion of the process of proofing, although her discussion is geared towards proofing a book rather than an article. She makes this suggestion: "Pay special attention to the following error-prone areas: chapter titles and headings, tables, numbers, proper names, foreign words, block quotations, footnotes, and bibliographies" (2010:202). In the case of an article you can substitute "section titles" for chapter titles in the above list.

The fun thing about proofs is that they always want them back *yesterday*. Actually, they almost always say something like "within four days of receipt." Even though it's inconvenient, take the deadline seriously, drop everything, and get them done. It's very important to get them back on time, or you could hold up production of the entire issue.

Congratulations, you've got a publication! Now, what's your next paper about?

Book Reviews

Finally, we come to a fairly minor form of publication, the book review.[54] Book reviews are a nice way to get your name out in public, as well as a way to get some lines on your CV. It's a good idea to do a few as a graduate student, but don't spend too much time on them, since they don't count for that much in the great publication game.

---

54. Recall from chapter 2 that there are three types of review: book notes, book reviews, and review articles. This section only covers the second of the possibilities, since that is the most common kind of review.

Most journals in linguistics have a review editor, who contacts experts in the relevant area to review a specific book. *Language* and the Linguist List publish lists of books they have available for review, and anybody can volunteer to review a book that appears on those lists. In addition, sometimes when a professor is asked to do a review, they may instead recommend a graduate student who they think would do a good job. Most journals do not accept unsolicited book reviews, and some do not publish reviews at all.

When you are asked to do a book review, the review editor will send you the book (which you get to keep—yes, a free book), and will give you a deadline and perhaps a word limit (e.g., 1000–1500 words).[55] Some journals also send review guidelines, but in my experience most don't. Check back issues of the journal to see what their reviews are like in length, format, and tone, and check their style sheet for style guidelines.

The purpose of publishing book reviews is to provide a summary and critique of new books so that busy linguists can decide whether it is worth taking the time to read the book (or at least can find out what the book says, so that they can pretend they've read it). Your goal, then, as a reviewer, is to provide this kind of summary and critique.

A very useful handout on book reviews has been circulating since Johanna Nichols wrote it in 1979. In it she says that a good book review is informative, concise, fair and objective, sympathetic, frank, scholarly, readable, and balanced. Some of these points are self-explanatory, but some deserve further comment.

- **Fairness and objectivity**
  Try to keep your opinions out of the review, and evaluate the book on its merits. If the book is written in a theory that you loathe, you probably should not be reviewing it. (Of course the opposite holds true as well: if a book uses a theory that you work in, you need to try not to be too partisan.)

- **Sympathy**
  There is no excuse for writing a scathing review. If the book is bad, your criticisms must be justified, and must be phrased in a sober, dispassionate way.[56]

- **Scholarship**
  You need to contextualize the book in terms of other works in the field. If it proposes a new theory of X, you need to know what the previous theories of X were, and refer to them in your evaluation.

---

55. Take the deadline seriously—if you're extremely late with the review, the editor is unlikely to ask you to do another one.

56. Nichols adds that if the book is absolutely awful, you might consider not reviewing it at all. Tell the review editor what the problem is, and they will help you decide what to do.

Nichols goes on to list the traits of a bad book review: the laundry-list phenomenon (just providing an unevaluated list of points the book makes), undue negativity, undue charity, missing the point, under-analysis, and being under-informative. She also mentions self-indulgence—remember that the book review is not about you.

Finally, Nichols says, "The best way to be a good reviewer is to be a good reader of reviews." This is excellent advice. Read the reviews in the journals that you subscribe to, or that are most central to your area of linguistics, and you will get a feel for what makes a good (and a bad) book review.

Exercise 13: Learn about Dissertation Fellowships

The goal of this exercise is to collect details about fellowships that would be useful to you while you write your dissertation. Choose three fellowships that are available to linguists.

1. How much time does each fellowship cover?

2. Is each fellowship intended specifically for starting dissertation research, or doing fieldwork, or completing the writing of a dissertation, or something else?

3. What are the application deadlines, and what materials are required as part of the application?

Exercise 14: Compare Two Reviews of the Same Book

Find a book which has been reviewed in a journal and on the Linguist List. (Be careful not to confuse a book announcement with a book review.)

1. Are both reviews organized the same way?

2. What aspects of the book does each review highlight as good points or bad points?

3. What can you learn about the book from each review that the other review does not discuss?

8 The Dissertation

This chapter and the next talk about the last stages of graduate school: writing a dissertation and applying for a job.[57] If you're still at the beginning stages of graduate school, these steps may seem far in the future. Nonetheless, you should read through these sections and think about the later stages now. What you're doing in the present is laying the foundation for what you'll be doing in a few years, and if you plan ahead things will go much more smoothly.

At the beginning of graduate school, the thought of writing a dissertation may seem preposterous to you. *Me, write a book-length work?!?* But once you've spent a few years learning the field, learning your area of specialization, and getting practice writing longer papers than you wrote as an undergraduate, it will not — I hope — seem quite so impossible a task.

One important piece of advice: make sure that your dissertation topic is something that you're really interested in. Remember that you're going to be thinking about this topic for a very long time, and if it's not something that you find interesting and stimulating, you are going to be very, very bored.

There are many extremely helpful books on the trials and tribulations of writing a dissertation, and I highly recommend exploring them. Most of the how-to-be-a-graduate-student books devote at least a chapter to the topic, and there are whole books entirely about dissertation writing: for example, Bolker (1998), Glatthorn and Joyner (2005), and Rudestam and Newton (2007). There are also many writing center websites (e.g., www.cgu.edu/pages/880.asp) that you can explore to get tips and advice. If my suggestions don't work for you, maybe those of others will. The point is to approach the process bolstered by as much help and information as you can get. Remember, you're not the only person who's ever faced the challenge of writing a dissertation, nor are you the only one to find it a daunting task. Just as others have gotten through it, you too will get through it.

---

57. The material in this chapter also applies for the most part to writing an MA thesis. Although I won't discuss that process specifically, it will be clear which parts are applicable.

The Dissertation Proposal

The first step in the dissertation process is to write a proposal, sometimes called a prospectus. Most programs have this as a formal requirement. Even if yours does not, I suggest doing it anyway. Tell your advisor that you want to write a proposal so that you can get feedback on the plausibility of the project before you start, rather than after you've put a significant amount of work into it.

The proposal should do the following: (a) state the topic of the proposed dissertation clearly (what problem will it address and propose an answer to; what phenomenon or language will it describe?), (b) state the theoretical approach to be taken, (c) state what language or languages will be used as data to support your conclusions, (d) say something about previous research on the topic, and (e) say something about your solution or approach.

What you need to get across is that you have found a problem to which a satisfactory solution has not previously been proposed (some solutions may have been proposed, but if so, you will need to point out their flaws), and that you have adequately prepared yourself to find a solution (if you have not already done so). If your dissertation will be more descriptive in nature, you'll need to explain as much as you can about what you plan to describe, and why it's worth doing. Either way, once you've done this you have a tough task ahead of you: you need to say something about your proposed solution or description, but of course you haven't written the dissertation yet, so you may not know exactly what you're going to say. You have to walk a fine line here. Dissertation proposals can't be promissory notes—that is, they have to be based on firm background research and solid planning. Yet nobody expects you to know all the answers that you will come up with right at the beginning.

Expectations vary about the length of an adequate dissertation proposal. No matter what the length, though, make sure that you have applied all your writing and organizational skills in composing it. Write it in sections, make sure it has a solid hypothesis, discuss previous approaches, etc. A proposed table of contents for the dissertation can be included as an appendix, both for your readers (to orient them) and for yourself (to provide a framework while you are working on the dissertation). Finally, there should be a bibliography at the end, to demonstrate that you have already started doing the background work necessary for an informed choice of topic.[58]

There is one last point to remember about dissertation proposals, especially about the suggested organization of chapters: they are not written in stone. I would be willing to bet that there has never been a linguistics dissertation written that conformed precisely to what the writer laid out in the beginning of the

---

58. It may even be appropriate to have this be an annotated bibliography; talk to your advisor about what they expect.

process. The organization changes, you suddenly realize that there's a side topic that has to be covered that you hadn't thought of before, you discover a wrinkle in the analysis that you hadn't foreseen, and so on. It is also very common to plan on doing far more than can be done, and to wind up cutting at least a chapter. The proposal is not a binding contract; it's a malleable and evolving framework that is there to help guide you as you write, just like any other kind of outline.

ABD Status

You may have heard others joking about the faux degree known as an "ABD." This stands for All But Dissertation, and is a fine status to have for a limited period of time. Problems arise, however, when students stay in ABD status for too long.[59]

For one thing, it's not good for your mental health. If your dissertation isn't getting finished, it's a good indication that something is wrong—whether it's with you, the topic, the process, or something else. The longer the dissertation stays unfinished, the worse it makes you feel. You need to pinpoint and resolve the problem, whatever it may be. (More on this below.)

Being ABD for too long also isn't good for your employment status. A prospective employer will most likely look askance at your record if it includes a very long period of dissertating. Expectations for the accomplishments of job applicants continue rising, and these accomplishments include just *how* ABD you are. There are so many highly qualified people out there applying for every single job that employers may prefer someone who already has their degree over someone who is still writing their dissertation (even if they haven't been working on it for an inordinately long amount of time).

If you are lucky enough to get an academic job while still ABD, you will find it incredibly difficult to finish your dissertation while you are undertaking your first year of teaching and all the responsibilities that go along with a new faculty position. Some universities reduce your pay until you finish, and some only give you a limited amount of time to wrap it up (usually a semester or a year). In the latter case, if you don't finish in time, you lose the job.

So there are many, many reasons why you should try to finish your dissertation in a timely fashion. The good news is that most ABDs do go on to finish, despite the ominous rumors you may have heard to the contrary. Leatherman (2000) cites studies which show that the majority of people who drop out of graduate school do it before getting to the dissertation-writing stage, and that most ABDs successfully complete the process.

---

59. A fun webpage which will keep you from working on your dissertation, "How to Avoid Graduation," can be found at www.ling.su.se/staff/oesten/undvik.

Getting Your Dissertation Written

Time Management

How do you avoid the "eternal ABD" trap? At the very least, you need to plan ahead and be conscious of time management to avoid this fate.

One strategy is to create a schedule which plots out how long it will take you to complete each stage of your dissertation. Obviously you can't really know ahead of time how long it will take you to write each chapter (or the sections of each chapter) and complete each part of the analysis, but you can make an estimate. Then, as you go, revise the schedule to reflect how long you're actually taking for each stage. You will probably have to do this several times. The point here is to keep yourself aware of the time that's passing so that you don't slip into the ABD never-never land where time passes without notice. The hardest thing about writing a dissertation is that there is no structure to your life except what you yourself impose (recall the discussion of this in chapter 5). This is probably the main reason that so many people find themselves unable (at least for some period of time) to finish a dissertation.

At the micro-level, you should also figure out a weekly or even daily schedule for working on your dissertation. In chapter 5, I quoted Lamott's passage on treating writing like a job—this is never more necessary than when writing a dissertation. Don't try to fit it in around your other obligations: this is your top priority, and other things should be worked in around it. Some people keep logs of what they do each day, and how much time they spend working on their dissertation. This can be a successful strategy for getting yourself to work, especially if you're the type to be motivated by guilt-producing approaches like a time log. (But be generous to yourself—thinking is work too, as long as it's not *all* you spend your time doing.)

One note of caution: common wisdom (often expressed in the many books on dissertation-writing) has it that you should write for four hours a day. This is great, if you can really do it. The danger of this advice, though, is that if you find yourself with—say—three hours of time, you may decide that it's not enough time to get anything decent done, and so spend the time doing something else. This can become a way of avoiding writing, and it's very counterproductive. If you can aim for a minimum amount of time every time you sit down to write, and that works for you, then do it. But don't let it become a trap. When I was writing my dissertation I found that sometimes I only had a half-hour in me, and other days I would go on a writing binge that would last half the night. Do what works best for you.

And don't forget to schedule in some breaks. If you make an overly ambitious schedule for yourself, you'll just ignore it. Your schedule has to be realistic, and you do need a little bit of time for exercise, recreation, and socializing. If you're getting writing done during your assigned writing times, then you can let yourself have a little bit of fun every now and then. Even the occasional vacation is possible—this can help you maintain your personal sanity, come up with a fresh approach to your work, and keep a healthy relationship with your friends and family. Just be careful not to let the time off stretch out into an extended period of time off, because the longer you're away from your dissertation, the harder it is to get back into it.

Regular Deadlines and Meetings

I usually require dissertators to check in with me once a week or once every other week. This can be in person or by email, and we set up a regular procedure for the check-in. I tell them that an occasional report that says "I did nothing on my dissertation this week" is acceptable, as long as it doesn't become a habit.[60] I require these regular reports for two reasons: first, it helps me to keep track of my graduate students, and second, it provides the students with a prod to get some work done. The theory is that if you know you're going to have to check in with your advisor, you might be more inclined to accomplish something. If your advisor doesn't have some similar method of regular reporting, you might request it. They may be shocked—it may be the first time they've ever heard of a graduate student wanting regular meetings. But they may also be pleased that you're showing the initiative to take such a step. The worst that can happen is that they may refuse. If they do, you may want to think about the quality of the advising you're getting.

Beyond just checking in, it's helpful to agree on deadlines with your advisor. These should be negotiable—that is, if you're really making progress but aren't quite ready to turn in a draft of a section or chapter, you should be able to postpone the deadline a bit. Such deadlines will have the effect of imposing a bit of structure on your otherwise structureless life as a dissertator.

One final note: even if the non-chair members of your committee have said that they don't want to see the dissertation until it's finished, it is nonetheless wise to have regular conversations with them about what you're doing. If you don't do this, and suddenly drop a dissertation in their laps two weeks before defending, you may be in for some unpleasant surprises at the defense.

Overcoming Overwhelmedness

You may become overwhelmed by some aspect of writing your dissertation. After all, there's a lot riding on the successful completion of this document. Dissertators are often fairly isolated, and this isolation can have the effect of

---

60. I'm grateful to Joe Salmons for suggesting this procedure to me many years back, because I find it makes the advisor/advisee relationship more negotiated and less authoritarian.

magnifying every bump in the road into a major setback. This is where it helps to have good communication with your advisor, and a good network of friends and colleagues who will help you get through the process (and provide you with a reality check when you need one). The key is to remember that although you have to be alone to get the writing done, that doesn't mean that you have to cut off all contact with those who can support and aid you.

Hopefully by the time you get to the dissertation-writing stage you will have established good writing habits and created a comfortable working space for yourself. If you haven't, be sure to do it before embarking on the dissertation. You will need a place where you aren't distracted by people, TV, email, computer games, and all the other fun time-wasters, because you're going to need stretches of uninterrupted time. If you have a family or a lot of roommates, you may need to find a place away from home in which you can work.

In chapter 5, I talked about what Lamott calls the "bird by bird" approach to writing, and this is a technique that you absolutely have to keep in mind while working on something as big as a dissertation. Here you will truly be overwhelmed if you start thinking about the enormity of the entire project. But if you take it in small pieces, and just concentrate on getting those small pieces done, you should find that it's doable. In the same chapter, I also described my dissertation binder, into which I put each section and chapter as I finished it. (I've done the same while writing this book, in fact.) It really helps to be able to look at hard evidence of what you have already accomplished when you're feeling overwhelmed by what you have yet to accomplish.

As I discussed in chapter 5, I work on the principle of ever-expanding outlines, filling sections out little by little, hopping from point to point as the mood strikes me. This is one approach; if you work in a more linear fashion, that's fine too. Most dissertation writers do discover, though, that the introduction and the conclusion really can't be written until the very end. You can sketch them out, but because the dissertation itself will change as you write it, the intro and conclusion will also change. So don't spend a huge amount of time at the beginning writing an introduction—you are very likely to find that you have to do significant rewriting later.

You will find yourself doing a lot of rewriting, in fact. If you have a conscientious committee chair (and/or other committee members), every draft you give them will come back with lots of comments. Train yourself to think of this as a good thing—imagine what it would be like trying to write a dissertation without getting any feedback.

Chapter 5 also covered spew drafts, and this is a method that works when writing a dissertation just as well as when writing a paper. But again, do not inflict your spew draft chapters on your committee. In fact, it's more important now than ever to impress them with your professionalism, and to show them how you've grown as a writer, since they are most likely the people who will be writing your letters of recommendation when you look for a job. So polish up those chapters and sections before turning them in.

A writing buddy or dissertation writing group can be a big help, both in terms of getting feedback (perhaps before you turn in a draft to your committee) and in terms of moral support. If you don't happen to know anyone who's writing their dissertation at the same time as you are, your university's counseling or writing center may be able to help you. They often organize dissertation groups, and even though the others in the group may be in different fields, they can provide a great deal of help with the process.

If you're really stuck, a writing consultant can help you with various aspects of getting the dissertation written. Google "dissertation consultants" and you'll find lots of options. But remember that a consultant can't help with content, only writing and overcoming obstacles.

External Obstacles

Many external problems can also arise while writing a dissertation. Hypotheses don't pan out, experiments produce disappointing results, computers crash, advisors move and sometimes even die, partners rebel against your reclusive lifestyle, and so on. What you need to do is take such events in stride, regroup, and get back to work. None of these necessarily mean that all of the work you've done is just so much wasted time. Work with your advisor (or someone else) to figure out a way to make use of what you've got, and redirect your efforts on a more positive track.

Defending Your Dissertation

I went through a very unusual PhD program, which didn't (at that time) have a dissertation defense. Although most people find the defense a stressful occasion, I think that omitting it was a mistake because there was no closure to the experience. I turned my dissertation in at the University's administrative office to a woman I had never met before, she said, "Congratulations," and I left. It was such a let-down! A defense gives you a chance to show off all the hard work you've put in and your great arguments and results, and you should approach it feeling jubilant and proud. Now, I know that's hard, because it will probably feel like yet another hurdle and yet another exam to pass, but I've heard from many people that a positive attitude can actually turn it into an enjoyable experience.

Your advisor has an obligation here, too. Quite simply, he or she should not let you defend until you're ready. I have been at a very few disastrous defenses where the student did not pass, and the sense of all present was that the defense should not have been held. So if your advisor is doing their job, you don't need to fear failure.

Defenses vary greatly across departments. Usually there is a presentation by the student followed by a question period, and generally defenses are open to the public. (I've never seen anyone but faculty, other graduate students, and possibly a partner show up). The presentation should be like a job talk, but the length will vary by departmental tradition. Talk with your advisor and find out what the norm is in your department. A good way to do this is to attend the defenses of other graduate students in your program.

Prepare for your defense like you would any presentation, including doing rehearsals. Check in with your committee members, and ask them if there's any area they think you need extra preparation in. They may let you know at least some general points they plan to question you on.

When you're ready to defend, prepare a carefully organized talk and a concise, professional-looking handout and/or PowerPoint presentation. Reread your dissertation from start to finish so that you remember what you said and are prepared for any and all questions. And then try to enjoy this closing act of your graduate career.

Exercise 15: Turn a Dissertation Abstract into a Proposal

Find a dissertation recently completed by someone in your program. The abstract at the beginning of the dissertation should provide an overview of the project. Without looking through the dissertation in detail, write a two-page proposal based on this abstract as if this were going to be your dissertation. You may need to read the introduction and conclusion of the dissertation for more information about the research if the abstract is very short. Answer the following questions in the proposal you write:

1. What are the primary questions that you would want to answer?

2. What sort of data would you need to collect?

3. What chapters would you include? Make a brief outline.

Exercise 16: Dissertation Proposals

Find two dissertation proposals that were recently accepted by your department. Ask some dissertators (people writing dissertations) or faculty if they would be willing to show you examples.

1. Evaluate the content of the proposals with respect to how much the author had already done and already knew at the time of the proposal vs. what they proposed to do in the dissertation.

2. How specific was each author about how the dissertation would be organized?

9 The Job Hunt

John Darley and Mark Zanna on Hiring in Academia
The academic hiring system is not a model of efficiency. The people making the hiring decisions are faculty members who have backed into taking that responsibility. They are overloaded, they are not professionals at hiring, and they tend not to be completely organized. They are also probably somewhat embarrassed at having such great decision-making power over other people's lives. (Darley and Zanna 2004:38)

It might seem like the logical progression of events would be to finish your dissertation and then apply for a job, but this is not actually how it usually happens. Instead, you find yourself in the midst of job applications right when you're trying to get as much as possible done on your dissertation, and can't afford to take a lot of time off. In fact, I remember when I first went on the market saying to my friends that applying for jobs was like a full-time job itself. So be forewarned—the application and interview process is a long and arduous one. This chapter will give you some advice on how to prepare for the strange world of the academic job hunt.

I start by describing the CV, the document that will be central to your applications. I then move on to the various stages of the application process itself.

The Curriculum Vitae (CV)

A CV is the academic equivalent of a résumé. It should be a complete and organized listing of your academic accomplishments and activities. Put one together on your very first day in graduate school. It probably won't contain very much yet, but you want to get in the habit of having this document on your computer and updating it religiously.

One issue I want to address right off the bat is what to call this thing. Most people refer to it as a "CV," which stands for "curriculum vitae" (Latin for the course or career of one's life). People also call it a "vita," losing the "e" in the process, which is fine. But when you write the whole phrase out, be sure to write "vitae" (it's genitive) or people will think you're Latin-illiterate.

The following are some general points to note:

- Spellcheck this document!!! Typos will make a bad impression.

- *Never, ever lie or exaggerate on your CV.* And don't pad it either. (Padding is the addition of items that really don't matter, or double-listing items, or generally just putting in items that are only there to bulk the CV up.) People can tell when you've done this, and it too makes a bad impression.

- In the business world, résumés are supposed to be short. In the academic world, the opposite applies: the longer the CV, the better (keeping in mind the caveat above about not padding, of course).

- Make your CV easy to read: don't use a tiny or fancy font, or small margins. Use a normal 12-point font and 1-inch margins so that the search committee can read your CV with little effort. Remember that they may have as many as 50–100 CVs to go through (if not more!), and if yours is hard to read, they may not have the time or inclination to try to decipher what you've written.

- Remember to revise your CV every time something changes. Keep it up-to-date so that you can print off a copy at a moment's notice. (This should become a lifelong habit, not just something for graduate students and job applicants.)

- Finally, don't waste money on expensive paper. In the business world this may actually make a difference (or at least it is said to), but I can tell you from experience that nice paper does not matter one whit when considering candidates for an academic job. (One colleague of mine goes even further than that, and says that a CV that's too fancy makes her think that the candidate isn't a serious linguist.)

Figure 9.1 provides a CV for an imaginary graduate student in linguistics, and the expected content of a CV is discussed below that. Note that conventions vary for applying for jobs outside of North America, including expectations of what a CV should look like.

Brad Student

CURRICULUM VITAE
WINTER 2012

Department of Linguistics   123 Main Street
University of Somewhere   East Elsewhere, CA 93770
1168 Happy Hall   (213) 555-1212
Somewhere, CA 93762   brad@student.edu
(213) 555-2292   Fax: (213) 555-8675

Education and Employment
2009–present. PhD program, University of Somewhere.
2009. MA, University of Nowhere.
2005. BA, University of Out There.

Dissertation
My dissertation. Committee Members: Chris Bigshot (chair), X, Y, and Z.

Publications
Under review. Nouns and Verbs. Submitted to the *Journal of Irrepressible Results.*
To appear. Language is Really Complicated. *Journal of Complicated Stuff.*
2009. A Really, Really Brilliant Article. *International Journal of Linguistic Brilliance,* 25(2):1156–1177.

Presentations
2010. Nouns and Verbs. LSA Workshop on the Parts of Speech.
2009. Language is Really, Really Complicated. Madison Informal Linguistics Colloquium.
2008. I'm So Smart. Linguistics Brown-Bag, University of Somewhere.

Grants and Fellowships
2011. University of Somewhere dissertator fellowship.
2010. Phillips Fund; grant for fieldwork on a really hard language.

Teaching Experience
Spring 2010. Linguistics 101, "Language," University of Somewhere. (Teaching Assistant)
Fall 2008. Mixtec 101, University of Mixtec Studies. (Instructor)

Service
President, Linguistics Student Organization, Univ. of Somewhere. 2009–2011.
Student representative, Committee on Make-work, University of Somewhere. 2010.

Professional Activities and Associations
Member, Linguistic Society of Somewhere.

Figure 9.1. Sample CV

What a CV Should Contain

There is no one right way to format a CV, but there are certain standard elements that it can and should contain.[61]

Elements of a CV

- Your name
- The words "Curriculum Vitae"
- The current date (this can be vague, e.g., "Winter 2012")
- Your contact information: address (work and home), phone, email, etc.
- Your educational background (from college on)
- Dissertation title and the names of your committee chair and members
- Publications, listed in reverse chronological order (most recent first)
- Presentations, listed in reverse chronological order[62]
- Current research/works in progress
- Relevant work background (e.g., Teaching Assistantships)
- Fieldwork experience, if relevant
- Computational expertise, if relevant
- Academic honors and awards (e.g., fellowships and grants)
- Memberships in professional associations
- Relevant service[63]
- Names, addresses, phone numbers, and email addresses of references

In a CV written for the purpose of a job application, it's acceptable to annotate the entries. If there are some important details of an experience that might not be clear just from its name or the title you had when doing the job, you can add a short paragraph explaining those details. So, for example, you might want to write a brief list of the duties you performed as a Teaching Assistant, or the responsibilities you had when you worked as a Research Assistant.

When you first start out, and don't have very many publications, it's acceptable to lump all types of publications together. However, once you've amassed a reasonable record of publication, you should start separating them out into subcategories such as books, articles, and reviews. From serving on search committees, I have found that I appreciate it when the candidates do this. If they

---

61. The *Chronicle of Higher Education* (www.chronicle.com) has a feature called "The CV Doctor," where they critique the CVs of two academic job candidates each year. Although some of what they advise might not be appropriate for our field, it's worth taking a look.

62. This may duplicate the publications section to some extent, which is okay.

63. Service (such as serving on committees) is the least important of your academic accomplishments, but it's one of those things where not doing it can hurt you much more than doing it can help you.

don't, I have the impression that they are trying to make their publication record look longer by putting the little items like reviews in with the items that really count, like journal articles.

Once you become a professor, you will learn about the all-important trinity of research, teaching, and service. These are the three areas in which one is judged for tenure, and increasingly job candidates are judged in these three areas as well. As you progress through your career, you may want to have major headings on your CV corresponding to these three categories.

What a CV Should Not Contain

Do not include in your CV a photo of yourself, your birth date, your marital status, or your life history (e.g., where you were born or grew up, where you went to high school). Personal information such as this does not belong on a CV. In fact, it's illegal in the United States for prospective employers to ask you about your personal life, and it's advisable not to volunteer it in the first place.

One last element that often shows up on CVs but should not be included is a list of courses you have taken. If you really feel that your coursework is important information for your application, you can discuss it in your cover letter.

Status of Publications

Obviously you will want to list all of your publications on your CV, as well as your manuscripts still in progress or in the process of being published. Be very careful about how you describe such works so that it doesn't appear that you're overstating what you've accomplished. If a paper has already been published, list it by date. If it hasn't yet appeared or hasn't yet been accepted, there are various other terms that can be used, such as:

- **under review** or **under consideration**
  Use this when you have submitted a manuscript to a journal or publisher. Also be sure to say which journal or publisher you have submitted it to.

- **to appear** or **forthcoming**
  This means that the manuscript has been accepted for publication. Do not use this if you have only submitted the manuscript, but don't yet know whether it will be accepted.

If something is in manuscript form but not yet completed, you can cite it as "in progress" or "in preparation." Some people list unpublished manuscripts in the publications category, but I find this disingenuous and consider it a form of padding. "Publications" means exactly what it says: manuscripts that are published, or will be published, or are being considered for publication. Put work in progress in a separate category.

Applying for Academic Jobs

This stage of your graduate career, like so many others, can seem insuperably daunting at first. As in all the other stages, finding out in advance how things work should allay at least some of your fears.

Before you start, talk to others who have recently gone through the process for tips and suggestions on strategies—they are the ones who will have the most up-to-date information on how the process works. Sometimes older professors, although well-intentioned, may not know that certain aspects of the process have changed since they were on the market.

The Modern Language Association (MLA) has a nice set of webpages under the title of MLA Career Resources at www.mla.org/resources/career_resources; you should read through relevant parts of it for additional advice. Keep in mind, though, that their guidelines are primarily intended for candidates in literature and related fields, so some details of the process as they describe it may differ from how it works in linguistics.

Figure 9.2 shows the steps in applying for academic jobs in linguistics.

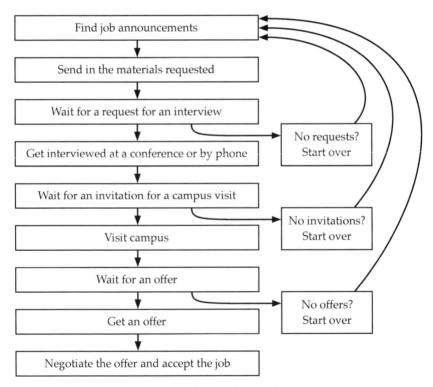

Figure 9.2. Applying for Academic Jobs in Linguistics

Stage 1: Applying

The first step you will have to take is to find appropriate job ads. At this point, the vast majority of jobs in our field (academic—applied and non-applied—and in industry) are posted on the Linguist List. You will also find ads on the LSA website, although the relevant page is restricted to LSA members only.

By "appropriate," I mean ads with descriptions that fit you. You may have to do a bit of a balancing act here. On the one hand, you don't want to wait for the perfect ad that describes exactly what you do, or you may wait forever. On the other hand, you don't want to waste your time (or the employers') by applying for jobs that you are not really qualified for or interested in. This is a point at which your network of mentors can help you—talk to your advisor and other professors about whether or not you should apply for particular jobs.

You will need to prepare a number of documents to send out—this is called your dossier. Each announcement will tell you what they want you to send, and there will be some differences across job ads. The minimum they will ask for is your CV and a cover letter. In addition, they may ask for names of references or actual letters of reference, as well as copies of sample publications. Be sure to send each department *all of* and *only* what they ask for.

I've heard that some professors tell their advisees that the cover letter should not be more than one page long, or that it should be exactly two pages, or other such advice. The length is really not the issue, though. What matters is getting across a good picture of who you are, what you do, and why you are the ideal candidate for the job. The last of these means that each letter should be tailored to the particular job you are applying for—don't just write a generic letter that you think should work for all jobs.

In a recent job search that I was involved in, I noticed two trends in terms of the organization of the materials that candidates sent out. Some just wrote a medium-length cover letter, containing all the relevant information. Others wrote a fairly brief cover letter, and then included a separate statement of research interests and, sometimes, teaching philosophy.

Whichever approach you take, the first paragraph of the cover letter should function as an introduction to the letter, stating the job you are applying for and giving basic background information on your qualifications. (It may seem silly to mention what job you're applying for, but remember that the department may have more than one position open.) The first sentence, then, often reads something like *I would like to apply for the position you have advertised in formal semantics*, or *Please accept my application for your tenure-track position in phonetics and phonology*, or *I am responding to your announcement of a faculty position in sociolinguistics*.

When you discuss your research, the obvious thing to do is to explain what your dissertation is about. If you haven't finished your dissertation by the time you apply, you should have a realistic timetable for finishing that you can present as evidence that your dissertation will in fact be completed by the time the job starts. Your advisor and others can help you out here by repeating that information in their letters of recommendation.

In addition to just describing the topic of your dissertation, you should be explicit about your approach—your theoretical perspective and other salient characteristics of your work. For example, if you did fieldwork to gather the data, and this is an important component of your research, you should talk about that. In addition, discuss other work that you have done, and try to tie all of your work together into a coherent whole. This can be harder for graduate students to do than for people who have been in the field longer, since grad students are often still refining their areas of interest and specialization, but do the best you can. What you want to get across is that you have a coherent research approach and a plan for your future research.

This is a situation in which it is very important not to give in to the urge to hedge. Have your advisor and others read over what you have written, and ask them to be really brutal this time. If you don't present yourself in the strongest terms possible, you won't get a job. Don't go overboard and make yourself sound like an arrogant jerk, but also don't underplay your real accomplishments and strengths.

Since most universities have a strong emphasis on teaching as well as research, teaching should be discussed too, either in the cover letter or in a separate statement on teaching experience and philosophy or approach. You should talk about what teaching experience you have, as well as what courses you are prepared to teach (and/or would like to teach). Tailor this to each position—make sure you've checked their course catalog, and know both what courses the job would involve and what other courses they have that you would be qualified to teach. If you've received teaching evaluations (as a TA or in any other position), describe what kinds of scores you got. You can add a few quotes, but don't get carried away.

In the closing paragraph you should indicate what materials you are sending, and you might state that other materials are available upon request (e.g., if they haven't asked for copies of publications or letters of reference you could offer to send those). It is also wise to let them know whether you will be at the relevant conference (for example, the LSA, the MLA, or the AAAL) and available for an interview. And you should do everything in your power to be at that conference— beg, borrow, or steal the money, apologize to your family, and go. Candidates who don't go to the relevant conference generally can't be interviewed (although see below about phone interviews), and are thus much less likely to get a request for an on-campus visit and ultimately receive an offer.

Be sure to send your materials in on time. Departments get so many applications that they may decide simply not to accept a late application. Even if they do accept it late they will wonder if this means you are habitually late on everything—not a desirable trait in a colleague.

As mentioned above, some position announcements request that you send letters of recommendation, while others just ask for the names of recommenders. In the latter case, they screen the applications and then request letters for some subset of the applicants. Either way, you should ask several faculty members who know you well (three is the norm) if they would be willing to write letters for you, and then be sure to warn them well in advance when you will be needing the letters. There are two ways of doing letters of recommendation: the recommenders can write a personalized, specific letter for each job, or they can write one generic letter which goes to your university's placement center (which the center then sends out for you, usually for a small fee). Other fields use the placement center method as their preferred method, but linguistics does not. If you have a generic letter sent it will seriously disadvantage you, so I strongly recommend against it.[64]

If you're going to be out of town during winter break, when many search committees are making their decisions about interviews, be sure to provide a phone number where you can be reached and the dates that you will be available at that phone number.

Do I need to mention that you should spellcheck and proofread your letter and other materials? Don't forget that the search committee is going to get a huge number of applications, and will be looking for anything that they can use to whittle down the pool. Mere typos will probably not be enough to get you booted out of the pool, but typos and other errors do send the wrong message. You should get a friend or advisor to check the materials over at least once before you put them in the mail.

Once you've sent everything off, you get to wait. Work on your dissertation, see friends, and try to forget about the job search for a while.

Stage 2: The Interview

If things go well, the chair of the search committee or the department will contact you to set up an interview at the relevant conference. For most linguistics jobs in the United States, this is the LSA annual conference in early January, although language departments with linguistics jobs usually interview at the MLA in late December.

The annual conference for applied linguistics is either TESOL or AAAL. Both are held too late in the academic year for most job searches, so departments interview at one of the other conferences (like the LSA or MLA) or hold phone

---

64. This is different in some applied fields, so as always, consult your advisor.

interviews. Now, I find phone interviews to be inferior to in-person interviews because they are less personal and it's harder for the candidate and the interviewers to get a good sense of each other. They are fairly common in applied linguistics, however, and they do have some advantages. Phone interviews save everyone involved quite a bit of time and money, the candidate can consult and take notes during the interview, and nobody has to worry about their appearance (you can do the interview in your pajamas if you want to).[65]

Whether you have interviews or not, when you get to the conference, find the placement or jobs room and register, giving your hotel room number and any other relevant information. This will help prospective employers find you.[66]

Assuming you do have one or more interviews, you need to prepare for the interview just like you would for an exam (this goes for phone interviews as well). Some departments regularly arrange mock interviews with their students who are going on the job market; if yours doesn't, you could request one. Failing that, at least discuss the interview with your advisor and other professors, and ask what kinds of questions they think you might get.

One category of questions will certainly involve how you fit the job described in the ad. There is the obvious question of whether you are, say, a phonologist, when they've advertised for one (but you probably wouldn't have gotten an interview if not!). But beyond that there are subtler questions of fit; that is, how your areas of specialization and knowledge would fit into the faculty and course offerings as they stand. Because of this, you should do some research on the department to see who the faculty members are, what their research interests are, and what courses they teach.

In the interview—just as in the letter of application—it's important to come across as having a solid research program. Insecurity may tempt you to waffle and say, "Oh, mumble, mumble, I'm just working on X because it's kind of sort of a little bit interesting." Don't give in to this temptation. It's absolutely impera-tive for you to state your research interests in the strongest of terms, positively, with a good sense of why your research is important for the field. Don't come across as arrogant; come across as excited about your work.[67]

---

65. With the advent of Skype, the pajamas may not be such a good idea.

66. Way back when I was interviewing, some employers had baskets where job candidates could leave their CVs, and they then scheduled interviews based on those CVs (possibly in addition to interviews already scheduled). This seems to be less common nowadays, but you should bring some copies of your CV just in case.

67. I was once on a search committee where we interviewed someone who was incredibly nervous. She was so nervous that she was shaking, in fact. But when she described her research she simply lit up, and showed so much enthusiasm and love for her topic that we were very, very impressed. In fact, we hired her.

One of my colleagues suggests writing up a brief paragraph stating the topic and importance of your dissertation, and committing it to memory. That way you won't stumble, or appear unfocused or uncertain about what you're doing.

Another area to prepare for is questions about the courses you would teach if you got the job. Think about *how* you would teach these courses—it's quite possible that the interviewers will even ask you what textbooks you would use for their courses. They might also ask about new courses you would like to create, so think about this beforehand as well. Think about courses of general interest, not just a seminar on your dissertation topic.

It's legitimate in such cases to ask what their needs and expectations are. If the department in question has a particular theoretical orientation or approach, you don't want to insist that you would teach a given course in your own way, disregarding their preferences. A little background research before the interview can help here.

A common strategy for ending an interview is to ask the interviewee if they have any questions. It's better not to be caught by surprise by this, and to have a couple of questions prepared. You might want to ask about the teaching load (if you don't already know what it is), whether there are teaching releases for junior faculty, what kind of research funding is available for faculty to apply for, what the tenure process is like, or what the area is like to live in.

Conference interviews are generally held in either a large room set aside for that purpose, or in a hotel room or suite occupied by someone from the department doing the interviewing. When interviews are conducted in the interview room (sometimes called the meat market), conversations from other tables can be distracting. Try not to let yourself get distracted or bothered by other interviews going on at the same time as yours. When interviews are held in a hotel room, the set-up can be quite awkward, since the rooms are usually cramped and there are never enough chairs. I've heard of interviews where some of the faculty were sprawled out on the bed, which strikes me as very inappropriate and uncomfortable for the candidate. But be prepared for some discomfort and awkwardness, and don't let the surroundings keep you from concentrating on the job at hand.

Finally, the MLA's website also includes an extensive list of "Dos and Don'ts" (www.mla.org/jil_jobseekers_dos) for interviewers and interviewees. You can only hope that your interviewers abide by the first part of the list, but you should read over the hints for candidates and think carefully about the points they make there. It's a very useful and well thought-out list.

Stage 3: The Campus Visit

After the interview (usually a month or more later, but sometimes even at the conference), the department will narrow their search down to a few candidates. These candidates will be asked to come to campus for a more extensive interview. Usually the department chair (or chair of the search committee) calls the candidates and works out appropriate dates for the visits.[68] The department will pay for your trip, but often you have to buy your own ticket and then get reimbursed, so be ready to handle this expense.

Once on campus, you will find yourself in a whirlwind of activities. You will probably have appointments set up with individual faculty members, students, the chair of the department, the relevant dean, and possibly faculty in related departments and other administrators, as well as having meals and social events arranged. You can always request certain meetings, such as a meeting with a campus childcare coordinator, but it's likely that your time will be tightly scheduled. Be prepared for a day or two which begin as early as 7 or 8 a.m. and end after dinner at 9 or 10 p.m. You probably won't get enough sleep because of all the activity (not to mention the stress), but you still have to perform at your best.

Two constituencies that you should be sure to pay attention to are the students (graduate students if there are any, and undergraduates, if you meet with them) and the staff. Some departments pay more attention than others to the opinions of their students, but you can't afford to be dismissive of them. Their opinions count! And although departments don't usually take the opinions of the staff into consideration in hiring decisions, a very bad impression might get back to the faculty and could as a consequence be part of their decision. Besides, the staff are usually the power behind the scenes in a department, and if you get the job you will want them to be on your side.

The most important event is your lecture, or job talk. Most people give their talk on the subject of their dissertation, simply because it is the research in which they are involved at that moment. If you are a year or more past your dissertation, you should talk about something you've been working on since you finished. The key is to talk about your current research, and to make it exciting and fresh.

Plan for the lecture like you would for a long conference talk—prepare an appropriate handout (the host department will usually make copies for you, although you might want to ask about this ahead of time), time yourself, etc. Such talks are usually around an hour in length—be sure to ask how long they have you scheduled for, and how much time should be left for questions. Also ask what the audience will be like, and shape your talk accordingly. You need to know if you can assume knowledge of technical details or a particular theory, or whether you have to explain such things. For example, if you're giving a talk for a position in an English department, nonlinguists will probably attend, and you will need to make your talk accessible to them. If you're giving your talk in a linguistics department, you wouldn't want to underestimate the audience's knowledge and insult them by explaining basic terminology. At the same time,

---

68. You might hear through the grapevine who the other candidates are, but don't ask—it's considered unprofessional.

you can't assume that everyone in a linguistics department knows all the details of some theory you're using, so you will need to explain at least some of the basic concepts. You need to strike a balance between clarity and assuming shared knowledge. Trial runs of your talk are very helpful here.

The department will probably provide you with an overwhelming amount of information about the university and the community where it is located. But prepare a list of questions nonetheless, and check it over before you leave to make sure you've gotten everything answered. Certainly you need to know about the teaching load, the tenure process (if it's a tenure-track job), salary range, benefits, moving expenses, and housing. Think of additional information that you would like, and ask questions. This is your chance, and asking questions shows that you're interested and taking the opportunity seriously.[69]

Stage 4: The Offer

Most of the time, offers are only made after all of the campus visits are over and the search committee and the department have had a chance to meet and discuss their impressions, so once again this is a point at which you have to wait. Occasionally an offer may come at the conclusion of the visit, though, so you should be prepared for that eventuality.

Make sure that all of your questions are answered before you even consider an offer. You may have gotten general information about various topics; now is the time to get details. For example, you may have gotten a general picture of what benefits are offered; now you need to know more about the health plans that are available.

The one point to remember is this: no matter how desperate you feel, don't say yes right away. If you are still waiting to hear from other places you applied to, you will need to find out your status with them before you can answer. But even if you don't have any other prospects, express gratitude for the offer and then ask how soon they need an answer. It should be at least two weeks. You will need time to evaluate the offer, thinking through the entire package. This is a period when you should feel free to make repeated contact with the chair—don't feel shy about calling or emailing with questions. Be polite, of course, but get all your questions answered.

I remember that I was shocked to learn that candidates are expected to negotiate their offers—it seemed, well, unseemly. It is, however, the norm. Some terms are negotiable and some terms are not, and it will vary depending on where your offer comes from. Sometimes you can negotiate the salary upwards a bit, for example, but sometimes you can't (some universities have salary ranges for

---

69. Darley and Zanna (2004:44–47) provide a long list of questions you should think about asking. Although they are writing for students in psychology, many items pertain to students in linguistics.

particular titles and can't go above a certain point). But as Golde (1999) notes, this is the one point in the job search in which *you* have some power, and you should make sure that you get as much of what you want as possible. She gives a good list of things to think about at this stage.[70]

This is also the time to bring up family issues. As mentioned earlier, departments are not allowed to ask personal questions of a candidate (although such factors often come out naturally in the course of the interview and campus visit), so they may not know whether you have a partner and/or children. If you are interested in a spousal or partner hire or other such accommodation, this is the only time that you will have the leverage to make it happen. Don't accept the job until you have this major issue worked out fully.

If you are waiting to hear from another institution, you should contact them, let them know that you have an offer, and ask when they will be making their decision. If it's going to take them longer to make their decision than you have to make yours, you are in a tough position. You can request more time from the place that made you the offer, but they probably won't give you much—maybe a week or two. At some point you may have to decide between the certain offer and the possible offer.

What if you're lucky enough to have multiple offers? Then you will have to weigh all the pros and cons about each place. Don't just make your decision on salary or prestige; think carefully about what will make you happiest. Maybe salary and prestige *are* what will make you happy, in which case you can decide on that basis, but location and other quality of life issues are also important.

If you decide to reject one offer in favor of another, let the department you are turning down know immediately. Not only do they have to regroup and decide what their Plan B will be, but there are also other people out there waiting to hear about the job you're turning down.

No Offer?

Don't contact a department to ask about their search unless you have another offer. It's horrible to be stuck in limbo not knowing what your future holds, but it won't do any good to pester the places you have applied to. Unfortunately, you may have to wait a long time just to get a rejection letter, because such letters are usually not sent out until the candidate selected has accepted the offer. It's rotten, but that's the way it is.

The MLA's webpage for job candidates (www.mla.org/jil_jobseekers_che) offers good advice and encouragement to those who find themselves without an offer, including the following:

---

70. Goldsmith also gives a list of issues to consider while negotiating a job; see Goldsmith et al. 2001:120.

- "You may be on the market too early." If you haven't finished your dissertation, you may have been passed over for candidates who were finished or who showed better promise of finishing by the time the job would start. This means that you will have a better chance next year, when (hopefully!) you will have finished or at least will be very close to finishing.

- "You may have pinned your hopes on too narrow a selection of schools." Did you only apply to the top research institutions, or to departments located in a desirable geographical area? We all want to live in San Francisco, but if you want an academic job you may have to settle for the Midwest (speaking as one who did this—and lived happily ever after).

- "New jobs [continue to] open up." True, there aren't many tenure-track jobs announced late in the hiring season, but many one-year positions open up late, and postdocs may be announced on a completely different schedule.[71] You may still get one of those positions.

- "There will be another job market next year." Next year the perfect position may open up. Furthermore, the next time around you will be better prepared. You will have had time to finish your dissertation, add more publications to your CV, get some teaching experience, or receive a grant you've applied for. Your experience in the interviews will help you to do better next time, and you will generally be older and wiser.

Don't despair: in the current job market it often takes several tries to land a position. And whether or not you wind up with an academic position, you *will* find employment: studies show that only 5% of PhDs are unemployed (Golde and Dore 2001:18).

---

71. Postdocs are short-term positions (usually one or two years) for people who have just completed their dissertations. They usually involve some teaching but are primarily a chance for the new PhD to do research. They are not as common in linguistics as they are in other fields, but they do crop up every now and then.

Exercise 17: Make a CV

It is far easier to keep an existing CV up-to-date than it is to write up your entire CV when you are busily applying for jobs. This exercise will get you started on this important task.

1. Create your own CV. Include headings for all of the required sections. Fill in whatever you can at this point, leaving the rest of it blank.

2. Keep this CV template in a prominent place where you work so that it will remind you of the kinds of things you need to do. Remember to update it every time you have something to add: a presentation, a publication, a degree, or even a change in address.

Afterword

Once you finish your degree and land a job, you will discover that the hard work is only just beginning. My goal has been to walk you through the most common stages of the experience of being a graduate student in linguistics, demystifying the process. There are two general pieces of advice I have stressed over and over again, and these will continue to be crucially important as you put your degree to use. First, nothing is set in stone. You may get differing opinions on how a process works or what you should do in any given situation, which means that you will have to use your judgment. Second, ASK, ASK, ASK. The key to succeeding is to get the information that you need. Once equipped with that you will be unstoppable.

References

Baron, Robert A. 1987. Research Grants: A Practical Guide. In Mark P. Zanna and John M. Darley (eds.), *The Compleat Academic: A Practical Guide for the Beginning Social Scientist*, 151–169. New York: Random House.

Basalla, Susan and Maggie Debelius. 2007. *"So What Are You Going to Do with That?" Finding Careers Outside Academia*. Chicago: University of Chicago Press.

Bauer, Laurie. 2007. *The Linguistics Student's Handbook*. Oxford: Oxford University Press.

Becker, Howard S. 1998. *Tricks of the Trade: How to Think about Your Research While You're Doing It*. Chicago: University of Chicago Press.

Becker, Howard S. 2007. *Writing for Social Scientists: How to Start and Finish Your Thesis, Book, or Article*, 2nd edition. Chicago: University of Chicago Press.

Bem, Daryl J. 2004. Writing the Empirical Journal Article. In John M. Darley, Mark P. Zanna, and Henry L. Roediger, III (eds.), *The Compleat Academic: A Career Guide*, 2nd edition, 185–219. Washington, DC: American Psychological Association.

Bergmann, Anouschka, Kathleen Currie Hall, and Sharon Miriam Ross (eds.). 2007. *Language Files*, 10th edition. Columbus: Ohio State University Press.

Bitchener, John. 2010. *Writing an Applied Linguistics Thesis or Dissertation: A Guide to Presenting Empirical Research*. New York: Palgrave Macmillan.

Bolker, Joan. 1998. *Writing Your Dissertation in Fifteen Minutes a Day: A Guide to Starting, Revising, and Finishing Your Doctoral Thesis*. New York: Henry Holt and Company.

Brugman, Claudia. 1983. The Use of Body-Part Terms as Locatives in Chalcatongo Mixtec. In Alice Schlicter, Wallace L. Chafe, and Leanne Hinton (eds.), *Studies in Mesoamerican Linguistics*, 235–290. Reports from the Survey of California and Other Indian Languages No. 4. Berkeley, CA: Survey of California and Other Indian Languages.

Cameron, Deborah. 1995. *Verbal Hygiene*. London: Routledge.

Chapin, Paul G. 2004. *Research Projects and Research Proposals: A Guide for Scientists Seeking Funding*. Cambridge: Cambridge University Press.

Chomsky, Noam. 1965. *Aspects of the Theory of Syntax*. Cambridge, MA: MIT Press.

Crystal, David. 2010. *The Cambridge Encyclopedia of Language*, 3rd edition. Cambridge: Cambridge University Press.

Darley, John M. and Mark P. Zanna. 2004. The Hiring Process in Academia. In John M. Darley, Mark P. Zanna, and Henry L. Roediger, III (eds.), *The Compleat Academic: A Career Guide*, 2nd edition, 31–56. Washington, DC: American Psychological Association.

Darley, John M., Mark P. Zanna, and Henry L. Roediger, III (eds.). 2004. *The Compleat Academic: A Career Guide*, 2nd edition. Washington, DC: American Psychological Association.

Deckert, Glenn D. 1993. Perspectives on Plagiarism from ESL Students in Hong Kong. *Journal of Second Language Writing* 7:1–18.

Fischer, Beth A. and Michael J. Zigmond. 1998. Survival Skills for Graduate School and Beyond. *New Directions for Higher Education* 101:29–40.

Geisler, Cheryl. 2004. *Analyzing Streams of Language: Twelve Steps to the Systematic Coding of Text, Talk, and Other Verbal Data*. New York: Pearson/Longman.

Glatthorn, Allan A. and Randy L. Joyner. 2005. *Writing the Winning Thesis or Dissertation: A Step-by-Step Guide*, 2nd edition. Thousand Oaks, CA: Corwin Press.

Golde, Chris M. 1999. After the Offer, Before the Deal: Negotiating a First Academic Job. *Academe* 85:44–49.

Golde, Chris M. and Timothy M. Dore. 2001. At Cross Purposes: What the Experiences of Today's Doctoral Students Reveal about Doctoral Education. Philadelphia: A report prepared for The Pew Charitable Trusts. www.phd-survey.org.

Goldenfeld, Nigel. 2004. Resources, Energy, Heartburn for Academic Physics, *Physics Today* 57(5):13–14.

Goldsmith, John A., John Komlos, and Penny Shine Gold. 2001. *The Chicago Guide to Your Academic Career*. Chicago: University of Chicago Press.

Green, Georgia M. and Jerry L. Morgan. 2001. *Practical Guide to Syntactic Analysis*, 2nd edition. Stanford, CA: CSLI Publications.

Harris, Robert A. 2005. *Using Sources Effectively: Strengthening Your Writing and Avoiding Plagiarism*, 2nd edition. Los Angeles: Pyrczak Publishing.

Harvey, Joan C. and Cynthia Katz. 1985. *If I'm So Successful, Why Do I Feel Like a Fake? The Impostor Phenomenon*. New York: St. Martin's Press.

Hockett, Charles F. 1966. What Algonquian is Really Like. *International Journal of American Linguistics* 32:59–73.

Johnstone, Barbara. 2000. *Qualitative Methods in Sociolinguistics*. New York: Oxford University Press.

Lamott, Anne. 1994. *Bird by Bird: Some Instructions on Writing and Life*. New York: Doubleday.

Leatherman, Courtney. 2000. A New Push for ABD's to Cross the Finish Line. *Chronicle of Higher Education*, March 24, 2000.

Luey, Beth. 2010. *Handbook for Academic Authors*, 5th edition. Cambridge: Cambridge University Press.

Macaulay, Monica. 1993. Argument Status and Constituent Structure in Chalcatongo Mixtec. In David A. Peterson (ed.), *Proceedings of the Nineteenth Annual Meeting of the Berkeley Linguistics Society, Special Session on Syntactic Issues in Native American Languages*, 73–85. Berkeley, CA: Berkeley Linguistics Society.

Macaulay, Monica and Colleen Brice. 1997. Don't Touch My Projectile: Gender Bias and Stereotyping in Syntactic Examples. *Language* 73:798–825.

Macaulay, Monica and Joseph C. Salmons. 1995. The Phonology of Glottalization in Mixtec. *International Journal of American Linguistics* 61:38–61.

Members of the Committee on the Status of Women in the Profession of the American Academy of Religion. 1992. *Guide to the Perplexing: A Survival Manual for Women in Religious Studies*. Atlanta, GA: Scholars Press.

Mitchell, Lesli. 1996. *The Ultimate Grad School Survival Guide*. Princeton, NJ: Peterson's.

Nida, Eugene A. 1946. *Morphology: The Descriptive Analysis of Words.* Ann Arbor, MI: University of Michigan Press.

Pecorari, Diane. 2008. *Academic Writing and Plagiarism: A Linguistic Analysis.* London: Continuum.

Perlmutter, David M. 1974. On Teaching Syntactic Argumentation. In Francis P. Dinneen (ed.), *Linguistics: Teaching and Interdisciplinary Relations*, 83–92. Washington, DC: Georgetown University Press.

Peters, Robert L. 1997. *Getting What You Came For: The Smart Student's Guide to Earning a Master's or Ph.D.*, revised edition. New York: Farrar, Straus and Giroux.

Phillips, Estelle M. and Derek S. Pugh. 2010. *How To Get a PhD: A Handbook for Students and Their Supervisors*, 5th edition. Maidenhead: Open University Press.

Pinker, Steven. 1994. *The Language Instinct: How the Mind Creates Language.* New York: William Morrow and Company.

Rittner, Barbara, and Patricia Trudeau. 1997. *The Women's Guide to Surviving Graduate School.* Thousand Oaks, CA: Sage Publications.

Rudestam, Kjell Erik and Rae R. Newton. 2007. *Surviving Your Dissertation: A Comprehensive Guide to Content and Process*, 3rd edition. London: Sage Publications.

University of Chicago Press. 2010. *The Chicago Manual of Style*, 16th edition. Chicago: University of Chicago Press.

Wang, Mary Margaret. 1997. Plagiarism. Handout distributed at public lecture, University of Wisconsin-Madison.

All website addresses in this book can be found at www.cascadilla.com/surviving.html and are regularly updated.

Index

AAAL (American Association for Applied
Linguistics), 25, 28, 88, 136, 137
abbreviations, 66, 68, 73, 77, 92, 93
ABD status (All But Dissertation), 82,
121–122
abstract. *See* conference abstract;
dissertation abstract; journal abstract
acknowledgments, 65–66
advice. *See* advisor; dissertation committee;
fellow students; professors
advisor
changing, 6–7
choosing, 6–8
co-advisors, 7
job search, assistance with, 135–138
regular meetings with, 123
research area, 7
seeking advice from, xii–xiii, 6–8, 16,
19, 20, 22, 32, 38, 47, 54, 76, 87, 88,
90, 91, 109–110, 112, 120, 125–126,
135–138
See also dissertation committee;
professors
affix, 60
afterthoughts, 71
agglutination, 59
American Association for Applied
Linguistics. *See* AAAL
American Council on the Teaching of
Foreign Languages (ACTFL), 26
American Philosophical Association, 43
anonymous review, 84, 111
See also review
applied linguistics, xii, 10, 25, 28, 88,
137–138
See also AAAL
applying for academic jobs, 134–143
Arboreal, 27
argue, 42
argument
data as part of, 33–34, 38–42, 49, 88, 120,
127

argument *continued*
evaluating, 19, 34, 49
making, xi, 10, 40–42, 49, 94
mistakes to avoid, 41–42
straw man, 41
summarizing, 19, 88
assume, 72
audience
conference, 8, 21, 83, 91–100
grant proposal, 105–106
job talk, 140–141
written work, 67–68
avoidance behavior, 76, 80, 82–83
Ayutla Mixtec, 62
Azuma, Ronald, 9

background research, 36–37, 53, 105, 120
Baron, Robert, 106
Basalla, Susan, 16
Bauer, Laurie, 24
Beard, Robert, 28
Becker, Howard, 10, 36, 68, 76–77, 80
Bem, Daryl, 57
Bergmann, Anouschka, 24
bibliography, 11, 14, 25, 32, 37–38, 53,
63–65, 105, 120
"bird by bird" writing method, 69–70, 74,
112
Bitchener, John, 10, 54
blind review, 111
See also review
Bloomfield, Leonard, 70
Bolker, Joan, 119
book review, 21, 114–116, 118
brainstorming, 22, 35
Brice, Colleen, 43
Brooks, Zachary, 1
Brugman, Claudia, 59
Bucholtz, Mary, 4
budget. *See* grant budget
*Bulletin Signalétique 524, Sciences du
Langage*, 30